John Kenneally, born Leslie Jackson, was awarded the VC during the Tunisian campaign, 1942–3. He was promoted to sergeant after the fall of Tunis and was later wounded during the battle of Anzio in February 1944. He subsequently joined the 1st Guards Parachute Battalion and went out with them to Palestine. Tempted to join the Israeli forces, thoughts of his wife and two sons, and his loyalty to the Guards, kept him from doing so. After the war he had a successful career and died in 2000.

'A wonderful introduction to the Second World War'

Max Hastings

JOHN KENNEALLY VC

THE HONOUR AND THE SHAME

headline
review

First published in 1991 by Kenwood

This edition published in 2008
by HEADLINE REVIEW
An imprint of HEADLINE PUBLISHING GROUP

2

Cataloguing in Publication Data is available from the British Library

ISBN 978 07553 1612 0

Typeset in Perpetua by Palimpsest Book Production Ltd, Grangemouth, Stirlingshire

Printed and bound in Great Britain by Mackays of Chatham plc, Chatham, Kent

Headline's policy is to use papers that are natural, renewable and
recyclable products and made from wood grown in sustainable forests.
The logging and manufacturing processes are expected to conform to
the environmental regulations of the country of origin.

HEADLINE PUBLISHING GROUP
An Hachette Livre UK Company
338 Euston Road
London NW1 3BH

www.headline.co.uk

To
Martin Peter

CONTENTS

This is a story of ten years in the life of a British soldier who was fortunate to serve in the two finest regiments in the British army: the Irish Guards and the Parachute Regiment. It covers one of the most eventful decades in British history, 1938–1948. It is a true story and is dedicated to those infantry soldiers who paid the piper for those who called the tune.

CHAPTER I

A CHILDHOOD

This is as I saw it, as I felt it, and I make no apologies for this . . .

I was born the illegitimate son of Gertrude Noel Robinson, daughter of a Blackpool pharmacist, on 15th March 1921. She was eighteen years old. My natural father was Neville Leslie Blond, Croix de Guerre and later a Companion of the Order of St Michael and St George. He was in his late twenties, Jewish and the son of a wool manufacturer. I was named Leslie.

In those days a pregnant unmarried daughter in a middle-class Lancashire family of considerable respectability was a social stigma of great proportions. My mother was packed off with £250 to a family friend in Birmingham and told never to darken their doors again. She changed her name to Jackson and I was born in Alexandra Road, Balsall Heath, Birmingham.

My earliest memories of Birmingham are naturally vague but by the age of seven or eight I began to take notice. We were still living in Alexandra Road, which in those days was quite a respectable area – the houses were fairly large, with gardens, and most were occupied by middle-class Jews.

The household consisted of Uncle Jack, Auntie Pearl, my mother and myself. There was also Mary who came in every day to clean up. Jack and Pearl were not married and I think he was a commercial traveller.

My mother worked as a dance hostess at Tony's Ballroom in the city centre. Pearl did not work. In later years I knew why: my mother and Pearl were a couple of fairly high-class whores. Pearl was somewhat older than my mother. She also had a son who used to visit her occasionally and who was a soldier in the DCLI (Duke of Cornwall's Light Infantry). He was a very glamorous figure to me, so smart in his uniform and clean and meticulous in his habits. He had got into some trouble in his youth and, as was quite common in those times, given the choice of Borstal or the army. Pearl was a beautiful woman – at eight years old I could see that. She was gay and irresponsible and the house was full of laughter, when she decided to get up. I remember her with great affection.

My mother was an enigma to me. She was a good-looking girl of excellent family, well educated, well spoken, but wild and with a devil-may-care attitude, both of which traits she passed on to me. In our years together I felt that she cared for me and loved me in her offhand way but I never got rid of the feeling that I was an appendage that she could well do without.

At this time of my life, in the late twenties, there seemed no shortage of money; I was well fed, well clothed and I even went to a private school, Calthorpe College.

Meanwhile my life at home was much the same. My mother broke her ankle which finished her dance work but it did not stop the succession of 'uncles' who came to visit her. Pearl too had her share of visitors when Jack was away. In my innocence I thought how lucky I was to have so many uncles who gave me coppers to buy sweets and keep me out of the way. My mother discouraged me from bringing other children home to play and consequently I was rather a lonely boy.

I spent a lot of time in other people's homes, especially Jewish ones. To this day I can recall what to me were their strange practices: the smell of the cooking, the darkness of the houses on the Sabbath, the strict religious observances, the fasting on various days.

One day Mary took me to school as usual, but when we arrived there was uproar; children and parents were milling about in the school yard, the headmistress was on the roof of the four-storey building shouting and screaming she was going to jump, and below a posse of policemen were cajoling her to go back inside. She jumped, and from the back of the crowd I remember a flurry of black bombazine skirts and a flash of her long white drawers – it was very exciting. I never returned, and the school was closed.

My mother enrolled me into Tindall Street Junior Council School. It was a tough school and discipline was very stern. Most of the kids were tough too. I was I suppose a 'posh kid' to most of my schoolmates, having had three years at a private school. I did not have the strong Brummie accent of the others and I had a hard time at first but I soon learned, and began to develop, a natural resilience which bore me in good stead in later life. Gradual acceptance came from the other kids and I soon became a 'rough nut' like them, much to the horror of my mother.

One day in the spring of 1930 I came home from school rather bedraggled and late; we had played marbles in the gutter all the way home. 'You are going on holiday to a nice farm in the country,' my irate mother said. 'Have a quick bath and put on the clean clothes I have put out for you.' I was bewildered, fearful and full of questions, and it transpired that I was going to Preston by train, alone. There I would be met by my Uncle William, my mother's eldest brother, and taken on by coach to his farm on the Lancashire coast to stay for a fortnight (which turned out to be four months). I was told to shut up, not to ask so many questions and hurry up as the taxi would be here in a minute.

The taxi arrived and my mother and Pearl came to see me off at New Street Station. My mother had put in my pocket a card with my name and address and the address of my destination, together with some money. When the train came in she sought out the guard, gave him half a crown and told him to look after me. I said my rather dazed farewells, very near to tears. Mother gave me one of her brusque kisses and said she would come in a fortnight to bring me back. Pearl was rather different; she gave me a kiss and a long hug and slipped a large piece of white paper in my pocket. It was a white fiver, a lot of money in those days. I still remember the sweet smell of her paint and powder and the feel of her white fox fur against my cheek. I never saw her again.

My uncle duly met me at Preston and we caught a coach for the long, slow journey up the Lancashire coast to the farm.

I was a little afraid of him at first; he seemed a very big man to me, dark-haired, going a little grey at the sides, and he smelt of horse manure. The coach stopped some way out of Preston on the coast road. We alighted and started to walk up a narrow rough lane which branched off. He carried my small case for me and when he spoke, which was not much, his Lancashire accent sounded strange to me. We came to a rutted track where an old tatty farm cart trundled up to meet us, driven by a big, raw-boned woman, with her hair pulled back tight in a bun – his wife. She looked very stern (she wasn't). On her face was no trace of make-up and she wore muddy men's boots. A great difference from my mother and Pearl's frills and flounces, paint and powder. It was not a large farm but they kept milking cows, a few store cattle, pigs and the usual hens and ducks. There were four large arable fields and plenty of grazing land, and Jem, their one horse and my sole friend.

My aunt and uncle were a dour couple with no children. However, as I got to know them I quite liked them and when my mother eventually came to collect her offspring they wanted to adopt me. The farmhouse was quite old and rambling – here it was oil lamps, water from a pump in the garden, and an outside toilet consisting of a shed over a cess pit. After the initial shock I loved it. From the back of the farmhouse it was only half a mile to the sea; it was a boy's paradise. When the tide went out I used to collect fish that were trapped in the rocky pools and inlets, mainly flatfish, plaice, etc. Occasionally I would find a large crab and I would glow with pride when my aunt thanked me. Sometimes when there was no work for Jem my uncle would allow me to take him on my travels. He was a very placid old horse and it would have taken a stick of dynamite under him to make him break into a canter. We would wander for miles along the cold and windswept beaches, picking up fish and bric-à-brac that the tides brought in.

The fortnight turned into a month and there was the odd letter from my mother. I cannot remember her writing to me personally. After a couple of months my aunt was becoming agitated about the amount of school I was missing. I would lie in bed at night and listen to them discussing me. The last thing I wanted was to go to school. I was warm, well fed and happy, and had new adventures every day.

It had to end, and it did. A small two-seater coupé came trundling up the farm track. It was my mother and her latest paramour, who had come to collect me. I was broken and reluctant to leave my aunt and uncle and Jem. The car had what we used to call a 'dickie seat' and I sat in that, very dispirited, all the way back to Birmingham.

We did not go back to Alexandra Road but to some rooms my mother had rented a few streets away, with no Pearl and no Mary. Everything had changed. Some puritanical neighbours had complained to the local police about the goings on at Alexandra Road and they were accused of keeping a 'disorderly house'. Pearl gave up the tenancy and moved to the Bristol area.

The *Dolce Vita* being over, my mother started to get her life into some sort of order. The first thing she did was to take my father to court and obtain a maintenance order against him for my upkeep. I do not know if my father had helped mother prior to this; she was always very reticent with information when speaking of him.

My mother started a ladies' hairdressing business in Mary Street. I renewed my relationship with Mary, and her children Frank and Marie, and returned to Tindall Street School. A settled life was good for me and I did well at school without trying too hard. I loved sport, especially athletics, and the love of sport has stayed with me all my life.

The hairdressing shop just about kept us going. There was never any money to spare and my mother's taste for the good things in life never changed. She went out most nights and went away occasionally for a couple of days with her latest lover. At such times I would stay with Mary, and Marie, being older than me, would look after the shop.

I began to get rather wild and undisciplined, often playing truant with other boys, especially in the summer months. We would roam the streets of Birmingham getting into all sorts of trouble, and my fleetness of foot served me well in getting me away from irate shopkeepers and policemen. We used to 'scrump' apples, steal bread and cakes from crowded shops, take milk off steps and crates of empty beer bottles from one pub back yard and cash them in at another.

Betting in these times was illegal and I had a 'permanent' Saturday morning job of collecting small bets in small leather satchels from various pubs and back houses in the Mary Street area. I would deliver them to the bookie who lived in a posh house about a mile away. He had a big refectory table on which he would empty the cases; it would be over-flowing with money wrapped up in betting slips. He used to give us boys, there were three of us, two shillings, or, if he was doing well, half a crown, each for our services. We would blow it on going to the pictures and fish and chip suppers. We had a great time. I was ten years old and very street-wise.

At school I was caned hard and often for my absences and for my general bad behaviour. It all culminated in a visit to my mother by the school inspector and a subsequent visit to the headmaster.

In this visit it was made plain that I was a bad boy and

it was wicked of me to cause my mother so much heartache (at which remark my mother started to cry — she was a good crier) and what a pity it was that I had shown so much academic promise which was going to waste. If I would attend school regularly and work hard I would pass for the Grammar School. My mother assured the headmaster that things would change, that he would have no more trouble with me and that she would ensure that I attended school.

At home there were the usual recriminations and scoldings, the outcome of which was if I would study hard and pass the Grammar exam she would buy me a brand new bike (something I had always yearned for). Of this I was a little dubious — I had had some of her promises before. However, I attended school, apart from the occasional lapse, and put in some effort; I passed. I got my bike — a brand new 'Hercules', price £3-19s-9d — and I became a Grammar School boy at King Edward's School, Five Ways, Birmingham.

In 1932 Grammar Schools were fee-paying. Everything had to be supplied by the scholar: cap and blazer, all books (which came to a tidy sum), rugger kit, PT kit, etc. We were poor and as there was no way my mother could afford all these necessary things, she got in touch with my father. It was the first time I was to meet him. He was a tallish, dark-haired man, and what impressed me most was the camel-hair coat he was wearing and the flashy, black and cream saloon that was outside. He was 'gentry'. He came up trumps and I was kitted out with everything necessary. It was another eleven years before I saw him again.

At King Edward's I was middle of the class academically. Sport was my forte and I represented the school through the 4th, 3rd, 2nd and 1st teams at athletics and swimming. I joined the school cadets and had my first taste of ill-fitting khaki uniform and rudimentary drill. We formed fours in those days, learned to shoot and how to put on puttees — we had great fun.

It was a habit of mine to go swimming twice a week and it was here I met my first real friend, Albert Tipping ('Tipp'), a close friendship with one lad that was to last for many years. We were both eleven at the time and he introduced me to a Boy Scout Troop attached to a Methodist Church in Birmingham. We learnt to camp and to cook, how to light fires, first aid, morse and semaphore — all sorts of varied skills. With great pride I won my first class badge, became a Patrol Leader and picked up my green cord for twelve skills.

Time was marching on and I was approaching my matriculation year. Tipp had left school at fourteen and was working as an apprentice electrician. He earned a pittance and I was no better off, although I worked three evenings and all day Sunday at a petrol station. The hairdressing shop had long since gone and instead my mother had several jobs, none of which paid a lot. We lived in semi-furnished rooms, mainly in the Edgbaston area of the city and always moving on when she got too far behind with the rent. We did many a 'moonlight flit'. There was little home life. I did as I pleased. I was well able to look after myself and I did not go without.

In 1938 I matriculated with no particular merit in any subject. I was glad to leave school in July, get a job, earn money and make life a little easier. My mother wanted me to take a white-collar job so I became an office boy in a large engineering firm. I absolutely hated it and my streak of wildness and insolence soon came to the fore; we parted company with no mutual regrets. I had still kept my part-time job at the petrol station, the owner of which I got on with very well. He had lost an eye in the First World War and was a bit of a father figure to me. He had built a small workshop at the back of the station and wanted to expand; he offered me the job of running the petrol and sales side of his operation.

I jumped at the opportunity and took my first venture into the motor trade. I was responsible for ordering petrol and oil and the few accessories he sold, organising the two shifts and booking in work for the workshop. I learned very quickly and enjoyed the responsibility. My mother had had misgivings about the job at first but soon lost them when I was able to help her financially; the mainten-ance order against my father had expired when I reached sixteen. My employer paid me well and life seemed set fair.

Scouting still took up a lot of my leisure time but both Tipp and I were rapidly approaching the age when we would have to transfer to a Rover Troop. We began to look for something else. Girlfriends never came into our lives. In those days we were very immature sexually and like most young men of that time were just not interested. I felt – having been brought up by women – the less I saw of them the better. In the early part of 1939 the papers were full of war talk but the 'peace in our time' message of Neville Chamberlain assuaged those fears. However, the hoardings were full of posters encouraging young men to join the Army, Navy or Air Force. There was also massive advertising for recruits for the TA (Territorial Army).

Tipp and I went to a sort of seminar at Digbeth Town Hall where immaculately dressed army officers explained what it was all about. It entailed instruction at a local drill hall two nights a week, one weekend a month and three weeks' training in the summer months. We would learn skill at arms, drill, Physical Training, map reading, etc., and we would be paid at regular soldiers' rates for the time we attended. It sounded great and we were very interested. It boiled down to two choices, a TA Battalion attached to the Royal Warwicks or a Battery of the Royal Artillery.

I took the advice of my boss, 'Don't join the bloody infantry, all that muck and mud and you march everywhere. Join the RA and you will ride.' We had visions of riding big powerful horses and wearing breeches and spurs. So in January 1939, coming up to my eighteenth birthday, Tipp and I joined a TA Battery of Twenty-five Pounders and I started a love affair with the British Army which has lasted to this day.

CHAPTER 2

THE START OF A LOVE AFFAIR

Like a lot of young men of our generation we were not politically conscious; the only parts of a newspaper we read were the sports pages. Our lives were full of work and the TA. We had only just been issued with our uniforms which were of World War I type: tunic and riding breeches with the long puttees, no spurs (much to our disappointment), the flat service cap and the usual denim fatigue dress and soft cap, also the heavy webbing equipment and fifty-six pound packs of those times. Strangely, we were also issued with the artilleryman's leather bandoliers, for which we never found any use. Battle dress was to come much later. We went gaily off to training in the middle of August. The camp was about ten miles from Barmouth in North Wales and was staffed by regular army Instructors who were very different from our own slightly amateurish officers and NCOs.

The Battery Commander had seen some service. He had a couple of medal ribbons as did the Battery Sgt Major, who wore the North West Frontier campaign medal. There was a sprinkling of ex-regulars amongst the NCOs, but all the sub-alterns were amateurs. However, it was all good fun and Tipp and I enjoyed the holiday. Discipline was not hard and so long as you looked after your kit, kept clean, did as you were ordered, paid attention and saluted all the officers, you could not go wrong.

It was a glorious summer; the tents were dry and the food was good and we had trips to Barmouth. Life was great, then the bombshell dropped. In late August 1939 the British Army was mobilised and on 3rd September war was declared on Nazi Germany. We all became regular soldiers from that date and I was on the threshold of a great adventure.

Chaos reigned at the camp: there was much tooing and froing with dispatch riders tearing up and down, and a general air of urgency prevailed. We were all confined to camp, and after two newly married erstwhile Gunners went 'over the wall' we had to parade twice a day for roll call. A new Battery Commander and Battery Sgt Major arrived and discipline tightened up dramatically. Guards were placed at all four corners of the camp, the whole perimeter was patrolled and we were on guard or picket duty every other night. What had started out as a bit of a lark was now deadly serious. The powers-that-be started to sort us out. We were issued with AB64s, the personalised little red book that every soldier in the British Army had to carry at all times. It detailed everything about the soldier concerned: regimental no., height, weight, date of birth, where he enlisted, next of kin, etc., and on the back page was the soldier's Last Will and Testament which we had to fill in. I naturally named my mother. We were also issued with red identity discs stamped with name and number which we wore around our necks on a piece of string.

The pay structure was also sorted out; the married amongst us had to produce their marriage certificates and their wives were paid marriage allowance As a young single soldier with no special military skills I was paid two shillings a day, fourteen shillings a week, of which we were strongly advised to pay our mothers an allowance of four shillings so that when and if we went on leave we would have some money to go home to. Not if you knew my mother, I thought, I bet she'll have a few drinks on me with that. However, I signed for her allowance. My friend Tipp did the same.

Our camp was enlarging rapidly and real training began. There was a big influx of TA and Yeomanry units, also Regular Army officers and senior NCO military instructors, and we embarked on a twelve-week crash course. This was the period of the 'Phoney War'.

It was at this time that the seeds of disillusionment with the RA began to appear in my mind. Those amongst us, and there were quite a few, who had affluent parents and connections began to disappear discreetly on OCTU courses to become officers. I could not tell them that my father had been an officer in the 'Blues' and had the Croix de Geurre, and I had no affluent family to support me. There were some Regular Officers, not many but some, who treated we ordinary private soldiers as absolute dumbos. Any man who has carried a pack will soon tell which officers had reached their rank by dint of wealth and privilege alone. Make a pointed remark or ask an incisive question of officers of this type and you were immediately regarded with suspicion. Being young and at times foolish I began to develop a raised eyebrow type of insolence. In Kings Regulations it was a chargeable offence coming under the heading of Dumb Insolence. I suffered for it and it took me a long time to learn that you can't buck the army.

December was approaching and we were nearing the end of our basic training. We had moved into the new type Nissen huts which were rapidly being built to accommodate the 'Militia Men'; these were the first of the conscripts, and we 'old soldiers' took great delight in telling them the horrors of the British Army and of the Royal Artillery in particular. These men were all aged twenty-one and with the booming war economy were pulled away from their well-paid jobs to fight for King and Country for two bob a day. They were not too well pleased.

We finished our training and were due to be given fourteen days' Christmas leave. Both Tipp and I looked forward to it – our first leave since we had been mobilised – and spent our last week in Barmouth getting our kit organised. The new type battle dress had recently been issued and to our eyes it was horrible and very badly fitting. We were allowed to keep our old type tunics and breeches and we bought a set of nickel silver spurs each. With our polished leather belts and bandoliers we looked every inch like old-time Gunners. My mother was really pleased to see me: absence really does make the heart grow fonder. She said I had grown and filled out a bit which I had — I was a touch over six feet and weighed eleven stone. She had quite a surprise for me, too. She had obtained quite a good job for herself at the Midland Red Omnibus Depot at Digbeth and had no need of the four shillings a week I had allotted to her so she gave it all back to me in a lump sum. I had misjudged her.

She had not changed much. She still liked her drink and cigarettes and she liked me to sit with her in the local pub with her cronies. I think she was a little proud of the way I looked and that her lad was doing his bit. She was also secretly pleased that I was in the Artillery and not one of those common infantry men. I did all the usual things. I visited Frank and Marie, spent an evening with my old Scout Troop and called on my old boss at the garage. He gave me a couple of pounds to have a drink with him and told me to keep my powder dry; he knew the strength all right. I also did the traditional thing all soldiers did: I had a posed photograph taken in uniform.

Our first leave fled by and in no time at all Tipp and I were on the crowded train heading for Wantage, Berkshire. At the depot we joined a Twenty-five Pounder Field Battery. I went into gun crew and Tipp into the signals section. We were only there a week when news came through that the unit was to join the British Expeditionary Force in France in early February. We young soldiers were thrilled and excited at the prospect. Almost all of us had never been abroad and we had all heard about Mademoiselle from Armentières – we wanted some of that.

The unit immediately went into fourteen days' intensive training: the guns were zeroed in, we learnt the art of camouflage and how to get in and out of action at speed. The unit began to knit together and develop a sense of comradeship. Then the bombshell dropped. Fourteen days before the Battery were due to leave for France, it was announced that all men under the age of twenty-one were not going. The order affected about twenty-five of us and we were replaced by older men from the training reserve in Wales. I was terribly disappointed, as we all were, and when the time came we helped them load up and gave them a ragged cheer as they went off to war. We learnt later that the Battery got as far as Belgium and were among the first to be hit when the German Panzers broke through. They had a lot of casualties, killed and wounded, many were taken prisoner and the remnants came back through Dunkirk.

I was in for another shock: Tipp and I were split up. Those of us left behind when our unit left for France were divided into two groups, half to join the HAC (Honourable Artillery Company) based near London, the other half to join a Shore Battery based on Drake's Island near Plymouth.

I was to go to the HAC and Tipp was to join the Drake's Island unit. We both marched in and asked to be switched around, either way did not matter. The Adjutant was adamant. The orders had come direct from RA HQ at Woolwich and he was not disposed to query them; we must learn that orders were orders and we all had to obey them. Another seed of disenchantment with the RA was sown within me. Tipp and I were like caring brothers and it was hard to break up when we went our separate ways.

The HAC were a famous unit. They were raised in the 1600s to serve King Charles in the Civil Wars and had served the British Army as artillerymen in several campaigns until after the First World War. During the peace between the wars they had evolved into a TA unit of high quality; their ranks were mainly filled by upper-middle-class Southern County types with a touch of the 'old school tie' about them, and they had produced Master Gunners and Field Officers of the first class; they were almost an officer cadre. They were being put on a war footing and I was amongst the first of their intakes of young soldiers from all over the country. I do not think they viewed our arrival with any great pleasure; for that matter neither did we.

On the second day after our arrival they gave some of us five days' leave, no doubt to give their officers some time to sort our records out and decide what to do with us. I arrived back in Birmingham in not too happy a mood. My mother was pleased I had not gone to France. 'You are much too young to go there,' she said, 'all those bad women and everything.'

My leave was uneventful until the day before I was due to report back, when who should turn up but Tipp. He too had been given leave on his arrival at Plymouth; his was for seven days. 'Sod it,' I said, 'I'll stay with you.' We had a good leave together, and we both left Birmingham on the same day to our respective destinies, I to face the music in London, he to Plymouth. We were not to meet again for some time.

On reporting into the Guard Room, the Sergeant of the Guard immediately put me under close arrest and sent for the duty officer. Next day I appeared on CO's orders charged with being nine days absent without leave. What a dressing down he gave me. I had let the unit down, myself down, in times of war everybody had to pull their weight and do their duty, etc., etc. The offence was much too serious for him to pass judgment and I was remanded for a Court Martial. I was marched in under escort to face two long trestle tables covered in green baize. At each end stood the Regimental Colours. I had never seen Regimental Colours before. The President of the Court was a Brigadier resplendent in red tabs and medals. He was flanked by two officers of field rank who wore full service dress. At the back of the court stood about fifteen junior officers. In front of the President lay the 'army bible', the large red book of King's Rules and Regulations.

The proceedings were short. The Prosecuting officer read

out the charge. I had no choice but to plead guilty, and my defending officer made his mitigating submission. He did well. It appeared that I was a young soldier of above average intelligence with excellent training reports and had no previous military misdemeanours against me. I had been very disappointed at not going overseas with my original unit and on meeting an old friend and comrade whilst on leave could not resist staying another week. That was it; the court adjourned to consider the sentence and I was marched out. 'Guilty as charged' was naturally the verdict and the Brigadier then lectured me in much the same vein as my CO had done. However, in view of my youth and previous good conduct and although an example had to be made, the court had decided to be lenient and gave me a one-month military detention.

I was lucky. I thought I would be going to the dreaded Aldershot 'glasshouse' which all soldiers feared. However, with the vast increase in army numbers the place was full to capacity and I was to serve my sentence at a small detention centre at Wellington Barracks, Birdcage Walk, London, and it was here that I first encountered the magic of the Irish Guards. The Sergeant of the Guard directed my escort (a bombardier and a gunner) over to the Orderly Room where I was to be handed over and signed for. An Irish Guards Drill Sergeant came out and roared at us to stand to attention and immediately ticked off my gunner escort for standing in a slovenly manner. 'Jesus,' I thought, 'what am I in for?' He studied my papers carefully before signing them and dismissed my escort. They scuttled away, thankful to get out of that place. He then gave me the keenest inspection I ever had. He checked me from head to toe, front and rear, and made me turn out my kit-bag which he thoroughly checked. I had always kept myself and my equipment clean and in good order. I had my years in the Scout movement to thank for that. He then clearly and concisely told me what lay ahead.

I was to be housed in cells at the back of the Guard Room with five others who were serving periods of detention. I was to do various fatigues every day including Sundays. I was to attend Punishment Drill Parade between 5 and 6pm every day bar Sunday, and Physical Training twice a week. These PT parades were taken by pukka army physical training instructors who were called 'Tigers' because of their hooped sweaters. Tigers they really were and these sessions were very rigorous. I was not allowed in the NAAFI and I could write one letter a week (which I never did). I was to salute all officers and address everyone above the rank of sergeant as 'Sir'. Did I understand? I replied 'Yes Sir' rather apprehensively, and, to my surprise, he was kind to me. He said, 'Don't look so worried son, you look as if you have the makings of a soldier. You have just stepped off on the wrong foot; you will soon learn.' I did.

They were large cells with a double bunk in each corner. I had two cellmates, both from the Royal Corps of Transport, one in for absence like myself and the other for striking a sergeant. We were later joined by a guy from REME who had illegally disposed of WD property. We scrubbed floors and tables, polished cooking utensils, peeled potatoes by the half ton, emptied rubbish and did every menial task that a large garrison barracks entails. The worst fatigue and the one I hated most was 'coal fatigue'.

This consisted of loading coal from a lorry into heavy metal bins and delivering them to the married quarters — six-storey blocks of flats situated near the barracks. The drill was to take a full bin to each quarter, knock on the door, place the bin in individual alcoves and take away the empty one. Being the youngest soldier I always clicked for the top floor flat. There were no lifts in those days and it was hard and heavy work. It was not the work that hassled me though, it was the women. Being a London Garrison married quarters the tenants were wives of NCOs and men from all types of regiments and many of them came from countries in which their husbands had served. They were of all colours and creeds, and those living in the higher flats tended to be the younger ones and they gave me a hard time. I was not really interested in women at that time. I had gone out with the odd girl occasionally, but nothing heavy. These women saw through me like a pane of glass and they teased me unmercifully; some of the obscene suggestions they made to me would make your hair curl. The more I blushed the worse they were and I dreaded going up there.

At first we joined the guardsmen on the punishment drill parades, but we could not cope. They quick marched, slow marched, double marched, they right and left wheeled, right and left turned and marked time with such precision that we were lost. The officer of the day wandered over and stopped the drill, looked at us with that bored tolerance which is the hallmark of the Guards officer and said, 'Take these auxiliaries back to the Guardroom, Sergeant.' 'Bloody cheek,' I thought, 'auxilliaries indeed.'

To my inexperienced eye these Irish Guardsmen were brilliant – their drill was so good, the reaction to words of command was so immediate, and to top it all they were so damned immaculate with uniforms that were well fitted and well pressed. Even off duty they walked about with that cocky air as if they were something special, and they were. I learnt that the 1st Battalion had recently left for Norway and the 2nd Battalion for Holland. These men who were impressing me so much were a sort of Holding Company left behind. If they were the 3rd team, what were the others like?

The upshot of our punishment drill parade fiasco was that we were drilled separately by junior NCOs who practised their words of command on us. I don't think we were very good for their confidence.

The month had passed quickly and we were waiting for transport to take us back to our various units. It had been quite an experience, my compulsory month's sojourn with the Irish Guards, and my thoughts went back to our faltering attempts to become soldiers with the TA. But I had learnt what the army could be like with the professionals. I resolved to do something about it.

Within a week of rejoining the HAC I put in a request for a transfer to the Irish Guards. The Battery Commander turned me down flat after listening to my reasons for wanting to go; his words were that it would be a retrograde step. In any case most of the original draft to the HAC were being posted to a Light Anti-Aircraft Battery based at Waltham Abbey in Essex and I was to be one of them.

The LAA unit I joined was responsible for the anti-aircraft protection of a nearby RAF fighter airfield. The gun crews were well established and they all had spare crews. We were supernumerary and did mainly guard duties and fatigues and were sent on various courses. On one occasion when I was on picket, a young lady arrived at the gate and asked for a certain Sergeant . . . Ever helpful, I said I would go and find him. In my naivety I asked, 'Are you his wife?' 'No, I am not,' she snapped at me. 'Is he married?' 'I don't know,' I stammered and turned away to fetch him. 'Oh, dear, dear,' I thought, 'I'm in trouble.' And I was; that sergeant gave me a hard time.

I was sent on a month's Motor Transport course which I really enjoyed. I learnt to drive the 15cwt Bedfords and Three Tonners and do routine maintenance. I came away with my white Army All Groups Driving Licence which carried an extra sixpence a day. I was a millionaire.

Dunkirk was over and the Battle of Britain had begun. I was to have my first tangle with the mighty *Luftwaffe* and have the privilege of seeing the RAF come into its own. The airfield had been strafed once and it appeared the enemy had used a canal about a mile away as a line of attack. We supernumeraries dug and sand-bagged gun emplacements each side at distances of about three hundred yards apart. We had nothing heavy, only two Lewis machine guns, mounted on tripods, to each emplacement. We had plenty of .303 ammunition and the large pan-type magazine. We manned these guns from dawn till dusk all through that glorious summer. We lay on our backs getting suntans and watched the proceedings in the sky.

There was not much love lost between the 'Brylcreem Boys' – the RAF pilots – and we 'Brown jobs' or 'Pongos' as they called us, but we were lost in admiration for their courage. There always seemed to be so few of them and hordes of the enemy as they clashed in the sky. We would cheer like mad as they downed a Dornier Light Bomber or Messerschmitt Fighter and watch silently when one of our Spits or Hurricanes spiralled down.

The losses inflicted on the Germans must have influenced them to try and take out the airfields and gave us our chance to have a much-desired go at them. They would come screaming in low over the line of the canal heading for the airfield and we would open up with rapid fire, using mainly tracer, aiming for the bellies of the aircraft. These engagements lasted only a few seconds but it was a great thrill and we would wait eagerly for the next wave. I cannot honestly say that we shot any down – they were long gone before we could know – but I did see tracer bullets snake into the aircraft and we did have the effect of forcing them to come in much higher, giving the heavy guns round the airfield a chance. We had no casualties but the airfield suffered, and the RAF lost personnel, both men and women. One entire gun crew was lost when it suffered a direct hit. However, the airfield remained operational all through these attacks.

The battle for air supremacy was over in our favour and after a lull we had the invasion scare. We manned road blocks and helped to build anti-tank traps as well as keeping up with our anti-aircraft duties. After the invasion of France, achieved mainly by the use of tanks, the army concentrated on anti-tank measures. We all attended anti-tank courses. We started off with petrol-filled bottles, then the 'Sticky' bomb which old soldiers will remember with horror. We moved on to the 'Boyes' rifle which fired a half-inch calibre bullet. This kicked like a mule and had a 2-inch rubber shoulder pad on the heel of the butt. We were supposed to aim at the tank drivers' observation slits and various vulnerable points. It was fairly accurate if you could hold it. We also did a lot of work with the two-pounder anti-tank gun – we became quite skilled with this and could get into action in seconds. However these methods proved, in battle, to be useless to infantry and gunners alike. It was not until the introduction of the six pounder, bazooka and the PIAT (Projectile Infantry Anti-Tank) that the soldier had any defence against heavy armour.

The invasion scare petered out and the enemy concentrated on bombing our cities. We were moved to the Dollis Hill area to provide Light Ack-Ack Defence, and from there I was to attend two further courses, the first of which was at a 'Z' Battery at Sheerness. The 'Z' was a new weapon. It was like a five-foot stove pipe filled with rocket fuel and explosive and electrically fired. In my day there was a single rocket to each platform and they were very scary – sometimes they would delay and as you turned to the mechanism thinking you had another misfire, 'whoosh', they would be away. Very scary indeed. It was a good job they were only trainers and not filled with explosive or some of us would not be here to tell the tale. Later, when they were perfected, they became a very good weapon. I have been on the receiving end of the German equivalent and it was terrifying.

The second of these two courses was at Watchet in Somerset. This was on the new 'Bofors' gun which was a rapid firing two-pounder light anti-aircraft weapon. It was quite accurate – we used to shoot at balloons being trailed by light aeroplanes. The pilots deserved a medal for it, but I can assure you we did hit the balloons.

On returning from Watchet I experienced my first bombing raid. I had seen raids before at the airfield. Being stationed near London, I had seen and heard them but always from a distance. This time, though, was for real.

I had to change at Temple Meads station, Bristol, for the London train. It was due at 19.30 hrs so I had a two-hour wait. I was lying in the waiting room half asleep when the air raid sirens went. I looked about me. There were not many people around and they seemed to be taking no notice. I did likewise, and tried to get back to sleep. Twenty minutes later I heard the anti-aircraft guns open up and then the roof fell in. Temple Meads station had a fine glass roof no longer. There was not a pane left. There were small fires everywhere and it was obvious the roof had received a direct hit from a cluster of fire bombs. The station was nearly deserted by now except for a few civilian passengers and the odd serviceman like myself. The really heavy high-explosive bombing started – the Junkers and Dornier bombers had a good target with all the fires blazing. A voice came over the tannoy advising everybody to take cover and for service personnel to report back in the morning as there would be no more trains till further notice.

I walked outside and it was not a pretty sight; the bombers were pressing home their attack on Bristol with a vengeance. Buildings were collapsing into the street, there were fires all over the city; the anti-aircraft guns were thumping away at their targets, and occasionally the silver and black bombers would be caught in the searchlights which criss-crossed the skies. Fire engines and ambulances were screaming about and I had to step carefully over the debris and water hoses as I searched for the local YMCA where I thought I might get a bed for the night. It was the first time I had been under fire; I could hear the shrapnel whizzing about and saw it as it hit the streets, sending up sparks.

I felt detached from it all. It was strange, just as if I was watching a movie of all this mayhem and it could not touch me. I asked a busy fire officer if I could help and he said, 'Piss off, soldier, get under cover.' He did direct me to the YMCA, though, which was only a couple of streets away. 'If it is still there,' he said. It was, and I watched the destruction of many parts of the city from its steps. After three hours, the 'all clear' sounded.

It was twenty-four hours before I left a battered Temple Meads station for London. I took the precaution of getting the Military Police sergeant at the station to stamp my travel papers to explain my delay. I did not want to repeat my earlier experience of being absent without explanation.

On my return to Dollis Hill I found a major reorganisation had taken place. Due to the increasing night bombing over central London and the dockland areas our guns had been dispersed to open spaces in a half circle through the Dollis Hill, Kilburn, Neasden and Cricklewood areas, usually with a searchlight detachment nearby. There had also been a lot of promotions due to the expansion of the gun crews. No promotion for yours truly: I had been transferred to Headquarters troop and earmarked for special duties. I was very disgruntled and slapped in another transfer request to the Irish Guards.

This was a different type of Battery Commander to the one I had met in the HAC and he did listen. I explained my reasons briefly. I had been on all these courses and received good reports, a lot of my contemporaries had been promoted, some of whom had less service than I. I felt I was getting nowhere and I wanted out. He turned me down but explained why: I had been considered for promotion but my 'sheet' (Army crime record) had weighed against me. I had been earmarked for further consideration. He also doubted if the Brigade of Guards would have accepted me with that blot on my character. He said I was young and impulsive but had ability and if I settled down all things would come. 'March him out.'

I was put into the MT Section and this turned out to be a 'cushy' job, much sought after by the other gunners. My duties entailed serving the various gun sites, delivering and collecting mail, taking out Part I & II orders, collecting any personnel who had reported sick and taking them to the MI room (Medical Inspection) – in fact doing all the myriad jobs necessary with scattered gun sites. At the same time I was learning all the highways and byways of that side of

London. I would have made a good taxi driver. It also meant that I was a free agent for some of the time and clear of authority, and it was in this period that I got into what my mother would call 'bad company'.

CHAPTER 3

'THE PADDIES'

It was my habit whilst on my daily rounds to stop at a cafe in Cricklewood High Street for 'tea & wads'. Here I met a group of Southern Irish lads who had come over to do manual labouring jobs, demolition work, clearing bomb debris, blacking out factories and all that sort of thing. It was hard and dirty work but they were well paid and had money to burn. There was only one snag to all this; on arrival in this country they had to report to a Labour Exchange to get an Identity Card without which it was impossible to get a job. Under wartime regulations this was very strictly adhered to. It also meant that with an Identity Card they became a registered person and after six months they were eligible for military call-up. A lot of these 'Paddies', as they were called then, did not want to know about the call-up, but quite a large number honoured their commitment and went on to give outstanding service to the British Forces.

Amongst these guys was a man named Halloran, with whom I became very friendly. He was about twenty-three, came from Cashel, County Tipperary, and was a real Irish charmer. He had actually kissed the Blarney Stone and was an out-and-out chancer. He had already received his call-up papers and was shortly supposed to report to a Rifle Brigade Depot, but being the free spirit he was, he had no intention of doing so. In a way he was right. He would never have made a soldier. The discipline would have choked him and he had no respect for authority of any kind, be it British or Irish.

It was February 1941 and the bombing of London was easing. I had settled into an easy routine of driving round the various gun sites and was bored to tears. One day Halloran asked me to call round to his lodgings in Cricklewood whilst I was on my travels and help him move his belongings. His landlady thought a lot of him and knew he had received his call-up papers. She had knitted him a Khaki pullover and balaclava and gave them to him as he stepped into the Bedford and waved him off to war; she was a good-hearted soul. He moved just three streets away. I was due for a long weekend leave and Halloran asked me to spend it with him. He was going to Glasgow the following week with a blackouting gang and we would probably never see each other again. We would have a few beers and go to a couple of dances and have some fun.

There was a large Irish community in Cricklewood and they knew how to enjoy themselves. We went to the dance and for the first time in my life I got drunk. Towards the end of the evening, and not unusually for an Irish dance, a fight started between some civilians and servicemen. Our group did not start it and the first thing I knew was when someone smacked me in the teeth. All hell broke loose and I discovered something about myself: I could fight. I had done some boxing in the Scouts and the TA and knew how to punch cleanly and protect myself, but all that had been very gentlemanly. This was for real and I punched and kicked with the best of them. My adrenalin was running high through the drink I had taken, and I did not feel any of the blows I was receiving. I felt great and was enjoying my first fracas.

The local police and the red-capped military police piled in to sort things out. Halloran, who in no way wanted to be arrested, grabbed me and with a couple of other pals we fled down the back stairs into the street and made our escape. We were all very jubilant; it had been a good night out. Next day I counted the cost. I had split and swollen lips, a rapidly developing black eye and various bruises all over my body. My uniform was badly torn, one epaulette had been ripped off and I had lost my RA cap which had my name and number on it. That worried me. If the MPs picked that up and went to the nearest RA unit at Dollis Hill I was a goner. I told my fears to Halloran and his pals. He looked at me carefully. I had acquitted myself well in the previous night's proceedings and I think they had a grudging respect for me.

'I don't know why you don't pack that bloody silly army lark in,' Halloran said. 'Come to Glasgow with us and join our contract gang. You'll earn plenty of money and be able to do as you please.

'How can I?' I said. 'I have no identity card and they won't take me on.'

'No trouble, I'll soon get you one. We want a spare driver, anyway and we can be away by Monday night.'

Desertion. I had never considered it; it was an alien thought. I weighed up the pros and cons. The torn uniform did not bother me, as I knew a way to get into Dollis Hill and I could put on my spare uniform and report into the Guardroom in the normal manner. What about my lost cap with my name and number in it, and what about my badly bruised face which would take at least a fortnight to clear up? What punishment would I get? The army looked severely on soldiers involved in fights, especially with civilians. A month's detention? With a record I might get two, and it would be the Glasshouse this time. With an ID card I could go with these lads, work for a month to get some money and then go and enlist in the regiment of my choice. I had no intention of deserting the British Army forever.

'I'm on.' I said to Halloran. 'Get me that ID card.' True to his word he came up with the Identity Card on the Sunday night. It was in the name of Kenneally, John Patrick, and carried a National Insurance number. It was all I needed and I could not back out now. Halloran had obtained the card from another Paddy who was returning to Southern Ireland and had no further use for it. Between them they fixed me up with some old clothes and an overcoat and apart from my shortish hair I looked an Irish labourer. With youthful bravado I burnt my AB64 in the grate. I despatched my uniform as I had my AB64. I regretted leaving all my few personal belongings at Dollis Hill but there was nothing I could do about it. Early on Monday morning, huddled in the back of an old Morris Commercial, we set out on the Great North Road heading for Scotland.

It was a bit of a nightmare journey, very cold and with regular snow showers, and we limped into Kendal in Westmorland on three cylinders. All the lodging houses were packed with lorry drivers and their mates. It appeared that there were heavy snow falls at Penrith and the main road had been blocked for two days. It was expected to be cleared in the next twenty-four hours. Not an auspicious start, I thought. A kindly landlady allowed us to sleep in her large kitchen that night and gave us a good breakfast next morning.

We looked a rough lot as we came out to the truck that morning, no one having washed or shaved, and I came to learn that whilst working they very rarely bothered. For myself, I was at that stage of manhood when I only had to shave every two days, but it was still distasteful to me not to wash and clean my teeth at least once a day – once a soldier always a soldier. The truck was frozen solid. I was not surprised: our driver, although a nice guy, was as thick as two planks; he had forgotten to drain off the night before and there was no anti-freeze in those days. I began to earn my keep. I organised some hot water and we thawed the engine out. I cleaned the plugs which were filthy, one of them being oiled up, and got a jump start from another lorry. The engine fired and ran sweeter than it ever had. Halloran promoted me driver on the spot and we headed for Glasgow. There was no umbrage from the previous driver; after the cursing he had got from the others he was glad to be rid of the responsibility. After an uneventful journey we trundled into the Clydeside area of the city where the steelworks we were due to blackout were situated. Halloran found some nearby lodgings (my God, they were rough) and at seven thirty next day we started work.

After a couple of days' work I pieced together what the situation was. There were eight of us and Halloran, who was the obvious leader of the work force. They had mostly been in England for ten months working on what they called 'blackouting lark'. They paid no income tax or insurance, they were paid in cash, and Halloran paid cash for any materials we used. They did not want to know about cheques or bills. They moved from place to place where the work was, living in the cheapest lodging houses they could find. Consequently they were all loaded with cash and building little 'nest eggs' for when they returned to Ireland.

The work was hard and filthy and at times dangerous, especially when working on the roof. The works foreman certainly did not worry about the safety of casual labourers.

He wanted every pane of glass cleaned before we painted them with the black 'gunge' as we called it. Halloran soon sussed the job; we'll clean the windows up to a height he can see and we'll gunge the rest. They'll be black anyway, he will never notice. He never did.

A couple of days before we completed the work Halloran had picked up on the Irish grapevine that the police were going round the factories checking up on all casual labour. Things were beginning to happen and the authorities were tightening the net.

'We've had a good run,' said Halloran, 'let's go home for a few months.' His pals were all for it. I think the money they had earned was burning holes in their pockets. 'You can come with us, you will be safe as houses over there.' I was pleased they made me the offer, but said no. I was going to enlist in the Irish Guards. They thought I was crazy but that at least I was going into the right regiment.

The lads told me the regiment was quite famous in Southern Ireland. During the First World War it was a common sight for an Irish Guards recruiting team in full regalia to go round the country towns and villages ensnaring young men to take the King's Shilling and follow the drum. Much, they added, to the horror of the mothers, wives and sweethearts.

I decided to go to the Army Recruiting Centre in Sauchiehall Street. There would be no point in going to England to enlist. If they accepted me in Glasgow I would save all that train fare. I looked in the windows of the recruiting office. They were covered in posters to join this and to join that and dominant amongst them was one extolling the advantages of joining the Scots Guards. Not me, I thought, I have not come all this way to join the Jocks, it's the Micks or nothing for me.

I looked at myself in the shop front window. That morning I had washed and shaved and the bruising on my face had almost disappeared, but my clothing was dirty and dishevelled and my boots were filthy. Ah well, I thought, I am not going in to ask for a commission, and I pushed the door open and walked in. I turned on my heel and walked straight out again. On the left, hidden from the outside window, was a long counter behind which sat a Recruiting Sergeant and he was flanked by two red-capped Military Policemen, who looked eight feet tall and stared frostily at me as if I had come to rob the joint. I admit I chickened out.

I decided to buy myself some decent clothes and a pair of shoes and go down to Manchester to enlist. If that took time and my money ran out I knew that my father lived in the Manchester area. I would find him and ask him to stake me whilst I waited.

That night my pals and I went out on the town and celebrated their goodbye to the UK. We kept out of trouble which was as well. Glasgow was a very tough city, and some of the pubs we went into contained the toughest characters

I have ever seen. The lads with me could drink but were as babes in arms compared to those Jocks.

We left Glasgow early Saturday morning. I was travelling straight through to Manchester, they were to change trains at Carlisle to catch a connection to Liverpool and Holyhead. They boozed steadily all the way down but I did not take a drink. I knew that if I had, I would probably have ended up in Ireland with them. We said our goodbyes at Carlisle station and as I shook hands with Halloran he slipped me a fiver and told me to look after myself. I did not see any of them ever again, though Halloran wrote me a letter some two years later. They were a great bunch and had been good friends to me. Although some of them were call-up dodgers I could readily understand their position; it was not their war and they owed no allegiance to King and Country and they had earned their money by hard work.

On arrival at Manchester I was lucky enough to get into the YMCA – in wartime Britain the accommodation was usually reserved for servicemen and women. I told the manager I had come to Manchester to enlist and he allowed me to stay. I slept nearly all day Sunday, a mixture of stress and tiredness. I had worked harder these last fourteen days than ever before and more importantly I was alone now and had time to gather my thoughts. Deep down I was ashamed of myself for deserting the Royal Artillery; being disenchanted with them was no excuse for walking away. My thoughts were very sombre; the police would be well on to me by now and they would have visited my mother to see if I was home. I reminded myself to send her a card telling her I was alright. I had not given her a thought. All in all I was not very proud of myself.

On Monday, full of resolve, I made my way to the recruiting office in the city centre: blow number one, they were closed, due to refurbishment, and opening on the Wednesday at 8.30am. I sat down in a nearby library to check my next move and my finances. The new clothes, rail fare and the night out in Glasgow had made a deep hole in my resources – that fiver from Halloran had been a godsend. If they accepted me on Wednesday there was no guarantee that I would get away quickly. There would be an educational test, the medical examination, and they usually waited till they had a bunch of recruits so they could send them as a party. It would be at least a week, a fortnight or possibly a month. No way could I last out a period like that. I would have to look for a job or alternatively I could search out my father and see if he would stake me for a few weeks. I chose the latter course.

I checked the Manchester phone book; the first one I picked up was for the Altrincham area and lo and behold there it was: Blond N.L. 'Shall I phone or go there?' I wondered. I had nothing else to do so I caught a train to Altrincham. It was a quiet sort of place and seemed like a large village. I enquired of a porter if he knew the name Blond and the house. He did, and gave me the directions.

It was about twenty minutes' walk away. I walked up the drive to the house, which was quite large and had a double entrance. I rang the bell and a woman who I presumed was the housekeeper answered the door. I asked to see Mr Neville Blond. Blow number two came up: 'I am sorry, he is not here, he is in London,' she replied. The disappointment must have shown on my face because she added: 'Mrs Blond is here, would you like to speak to her?' I replied that I would and she showed me into a drawing room to the right of the hall. 'What name shall I tell Mrs Blond,' she asked. 'Jackson,' I said, 'Leslie Jackson.'

I looked around the drawing room. It was beautifully furnished and immaculately clean. After the dingy doss houses I had been living in, this place was a palace. Thank God I bought those new clothes, I thought, I would never have got past the front door dressed as I had been. I was impressed by my surroundings but not overawed. 'Yes?' a voice said behind me. She had come into the room very quietly. I turned to face her. 'Mrs Blond?' I asked. She nodded and studied me carefully. I started my prepared speech. 'I apologise for barging in on you like this. My name is Jackson, Leslie Jackson, and I wanted to see Mr Blond about . . .' She stopped me in full flight. 'I know who you are,' she said quietly, 'you bear a strong resemblance to your father. How can I help you?'

I studied her as carefully as she had studied me. This woman was a lady. She was very small and slim: I towered over her. 'Shall we sit down?' she said. She had one of those accents that cost a lot of money, and was fabulously dressed. I took a deep breath and told her the truth about my present situation. As I spoke I noticed an amused smile on her face. 'I bet she thinks this is a right boyo her husband had fathered.' She sensed my relief when I ended. 'Now that's over we'll have some tea,' she said. 'Would you excuse me for a few minutes?' I felt that she liked me.

After a while the housekeeper came in with the tea tray. Even she smiled at me. I noticed she had laid out tea for three. Mrs Blond returned and apologised for keeping me waiting and proceeded to pour out the tea. The door opened and in walked a Major in Rifle Brigade uniform. 'Christ, she's shopped me,' I thought. I need not have worried. She introduced him to me as Major so and so who was on leave and paying a visit. He had been serving in the Middle East and told me all about it. I judged him to be a Staff or Admin Officer of some sort. I felt he was rather condescending. Maybe I misjudged him because of the shock he gave me. He did not stay long. We chatted a little longer and she told me she had two sons who were at boarding school. Not wanting to wear out my welcome I said I would have to go. She gave me twenty-five pounds. 'Will that be enough for you?' she asked. 'More than enough,' I replied. (I had never had that much money in my life.) She also offered me a lift to the station which I declined. On seeing me to the door she wished me the best of luck and asked me to phone her if I had been successful in enlisting.

As I walked back to the station I could not believe my luck. Many women faced with an illegitimate son of their husband would have shown him the door. She had treated me with courtesy and had helped me on my way. I thought how lucky my half brothers were to have such a classy lady as a mother. I did not meet her again.

On Wednesday morning I headed for the Recruiting Office in a much more confident mood than before. It is amazing what decent clothes and money in the pocket will do for a young man's confidence. The office was quite busy, with young men milling about looking at this and that. There were the usual three counters: Army, Navy and Air Force. At the Army desk I told the sergeant, 'I want to join the Irish Guards.' 'That's what I like to hear,' he said, 'a man who makes up his own mind. Got your ID card?' I slipped it over and held my breath. He took all the details from it and filled in a large form. He asked whether I wanted to sign on for the duration of the war or take a seven-year engagement. I chose the duration.

'Sign here,' he said, 'and I will tell you the drill.' I signed the engagement form J P Kenneally. It was the first time I had ever written the name. 'You will take a short educational exam, you can do that now. The medical team will be here this afternoon. If you can come back and you pass the medical in A1 category you will then take the Loyal Oath and you will be in. How soon do you want to go?'

'As soon as possible,' I replied.

The educational test consisted of twelve questions; three simple arithmetic, and three each on history, geography and English spelling – a boy of twelve could have answered them. One word I had to spell was 'officialdom'.

The medical examination was very thorough but I had no worries in that respect. The MO gave me a slip of paper which he stamped and signed. 'Get dressed and give this note to the sergeant,' he said. 'You're in, lad,' said the sergeant, and gathered up all the papers. 'Come and meet the Recruiting Officer.' He was a Captain in the Royal Engineers, obviously of First World War vintage. He checked my papers carefully and then reached for a bible. I gave the oath of loyalty. He shook hands and wished me luck.

That was it. I had realised my ambition. I had joined the Irish Guards. I felt quite elated, but I did not kid myself that I was a knight in shining white armour. The plain facts were that I had deserted one regiment for another and in the process had picked up a new identity to cover my tracks. I comforted myself with the thought that it was under four weeks ago that I had left the Royal Artillery and here I was back in the army again; I was not too bad a deserter. Those past four weeks seemed like four years to me. I resolved to put it all behind me and take advantage of the fresh start that fate had given me.

My orders were to report to the Recruiting Centre on the following Monday and I would be given travel instructions. During the weekend I phoned Mrs Blond as promised. She wished me bon voyage. I also wrote to my mother and Tipp; there was no one else who would be interested.

CHAPTER 4

THE MAKING OF A GUARDSMAN

Sharp at 8.30am on Monday I joined a number of other young men to receive my travel orders. We were to go by army transport to Lime Street Station, Liverpool, where we would be given Railway Warrants to travel to our various destinations. At Liverpool our number increased and they sorted us out in Regiments — there were but six of us for the Brigade of Guards and we were to go to the Guards Depot at Caterham in Surrey. The journey to Caterham was uneventful; we did not have much to say to each other, each one busy with his own thoughts. At the station we looked about us not knowing which way to go. Without being asked, the station master said: 'Up the road, about a mile, you won't miss it.' He must have seen hundreds of young men like us.

He was right, we could not miss it. As we walked up the hill we heard martial music being played – the various bands were practising. As we approached the red brick gates I thought the place looked like a red brick university. It was a seat of learning, but of a very different sort. The Corporal of the Guard rattled up a picket sentry to take us to our various destinations. I was to go to number 5 Company Irish Guards. I could hardly keep up with him as he marched along, swinging his arms shoulders high. 'Where are we going?' I asked him. 'Roberts Block,' he said. 'Can't we walk across the square to it?' I asked. 'Christ,' he said, 'you'll get us both shot. You always walk around the square, never ever across it.' Number One lesson learnt. At the orderly room I handed in my travel documents. 'Hand over your ID card,' the clerk said. 'You won't need that any more. You will be issued with an AB64 in a day or two.' I was glad to do so; that card had always felt red hot to me. Another guardsman took me to a barrack room and handed me over to a Trained Soldier.

The Trained Soldier was usually a much older man and a father figure to the young recruits. It was he who taught us how to lay out our kit, how to polish buttons and boots, to fold blankets to a millimetre in accuracy, and how to lay the rough battle dress trousers down, sleep on them and produce immaculate creases. He taught us how to scrub, clean and polish the barrack room furniture. The stove used to amuse me; it was not there for any functional purpose but as a thing of great beauty to be much admired – it was heresy to burn anything in it. All queries and questions we took to the Trained Soldier, who told us what to do and what not to do and pointed out the many and varied pitfalls we were bound to fall into. I also suspect he reported to the Squad Sergeant on the attitudes and possibilities of the recruits he mentored.

We were to be a squad of twenty-one; I was the eighteenth

to arrive. The other three reported in next day. We came from all points of the compass, Southern and Northern Irish, Liverpool, Manchester, Geordies, Londoners and one young Welshman. The first thing we were taught was how to stand. This was achieved by standing against the wall with our heads, shoulders, backsides and heels pressing against it. This is not as easy as it looks, and was often used as a quick punishment for slacking.

Next we were taught how to walk. Heel and toe, heel and toe was drummed in to us. We did many foot exercises to get our feet and ankles lithe and supple. Next came arm and leg co-ordination, which some of the guys found difficult. Then there was the physical training. I had done plenty of PT in my time, but this was something else — gruelling and exhausting with no let-up. It was not unusual to go to bed at 6.30pm absolutely shattered. At the end of our first two weeks Sgt Carr called me over. 'I have been watching you,' he said. 'Have you had any military training?' I thought quickly and quite truthfully told him I had been in the Army Cadet Corps for some years. 'That must be it,' he said.

We pounded the square for hours and hours; gradually, very gradually, we began to improve. Being pitch-forked into the crazy life had been quite a culture shock for some of my more sensitive comrades. There was no privacy whatever; we ate, slept and bathed together in the communal baths; it was no place to be shy or retiring.

The incessant drills and physical training went on and

the PT Instructors started to put some fighting aggression into us. The squad was divided into four teams of five and had to box each other for one round of two minutes each, which was long enough if you had never boxed before. The best five to emerge from these bouts were then matched with similar teams from the Grenadiers, Coldstream, Scotch and Welsh recruits. These teams would box each other over a period of four weeks until a winning team emerged. Weight and height did not come into it and each boxer took pot luck on who his opponent might be. It was my misfortune to survive the inter-squad bouts, only for my first outside opponent to be a guy from the Grenadiers who was bigger, older, much heavier and uglier than me. I sailed in with all guns blazing and managed to survive the first round. In the second round he caught me with a haymaker on the side of the head and down I went. My brief career as an Irish Guards boxer was over. This exercise was good fun and very revealing; men you thought were 'wimpy' turned out to be just the opposite, and some of the big tough guys turned out to be not so tough after all.

Time marched on and we were nearing the date of our passing out parade. We had developed into a good squad; the mutual suffering and experiences had moulded us together as good comrades. During our training we had to learn all about the great fighting traditions of the regiment. We were taught the various crests and the names of battles and campaigns they fought and we had to learn the names and ranks of those who had won the Victoria Cross. We began to develop a pride in our regiment and a pride in ourselves – we were becoming Irish Guardsmen.

The day we had been waiting for came along and as we formed up with identical squads from the other four regiments of foot guards our instructor Sgt Carr impressed upon us that we had to be the best and a credit to him. It was like a miniature 'Trooping the Colour'. The bands struck up and the pipers played, we marched past the Camp Commandant in quick and slow time to each regimental tune. The military music never fails to get one going, the adrenalin flows and we dug our heels in and swung our arms with the best of them. It was great to be a soldier and we did not let Sgt Carr down.

Next day, immaculate as new pins, we were formed up outside Company HQ and the Company Commander told us we had done well and wished us luck. We were all going to join the Training Battalion at Hobbs Barracks, Lingfield.

We piled into the transport, Sgt Carr gave us a nod and we were away on the next stage of our adventure. As we drove down Caterham Hill we passed some young men struggling up it with their cases; 'poor sods,' we thought.

Hobbs Barracks was in the middle of nowhere; the nearest civilisation was Lingfield, a small town by the racecourse, and East Grinstead, a very pretty small town about six miles away. The main emphasis at the Training Battalion was on

Weapon Training, Fitness and Tactics. We learned bayonet fighting, how to use the Bren light machine gun, the Thompson (later replaced by the Sten), and the 2" and 3" mortar. We were taught how to lay mines, put up barbed wire, dig trenches, etc. We had great fun learning about explosives and how to detonate them and blow things up. There was the usual grenade training with the Mills and the Bakelite smoke grenades. We learned about Poison Gas and unarmed combat, which was then coming into vogue.

Our training was very different from that of the infantryman of the First World War. The days of the mono-cled officer leading his men 'over the top' were long gone. We were taught to kill in a hundred different ways, nothing was too low or too dirty. We learnt the killing business, and it was deadly serious.

During this period of preparation the Training Battalion was commanded by Lieutenant-Colonel Lord Gough MC, a veteran of the First World War and a great character. The Colonel had a very well-fed Pekinese dog that was as old as him and used to follow him everywhere. It was the dog's habit to sleep between the sandbags surrounding the Guard Room on the hot summer nights. On such a night, at around 3am, a bored sentry decided to clean his bayonet and plunged it into the nearest sandbag: a yelp, end of dog. The sentry was horror-stricken at what he had done – he had killed the CO's dog. With the help of the other sentry on duty he hurriedly buried it at the back of the Guard Room with full Military Honours. Next day half the battalion was out searching the barracks and surrounding countryside. It was assumed the dog had deserted. One of the sentries was a friend of mine and when the hue and cry died down he told me the story. Years later I was to meet the Colonel's grandson, Viscount Gough, at a regimental reunion in North Africa but I did not enlighten him on what happened to his grandfather's dog.

One day, much to my surprise, I saw my name down for Company orders. 'What have I done?' I asked the sergeant-in-waiting. 'I don't know,' he said. 'You are not on a charge, the Company Commander wants to see you.' The Company Commander was Captain Simon Coombe, of Watney Coombe and Reid fame. Feeling some trepidation I was marched in to face him. 'Ah, Kenneally,' he said, 'I am considering promoting you to Lance Corporal and putting you on a Junior NCO course.' I had become a non-commissioned officer.

I enjoyed the course and came away with a good report and wore my two stripes with pride.

I was becoming a good Irish Guardsman – confident and skilled at what I had to do. I was a good shot, I played a lot of rugger and I like to think I was as good a wing three-quarter as the Training Battalion had. I had two periods of leave at this time. Having heard from my Irish comrades about the delights of that Emerald Isle, I decided to go see for myself. I applied for leave to visit my pseudo relatives in Dublin. I looked forward to it with great anticipation: it was the first time I had been out of the country. During the crossing I met an Irish girl who was to become a good friend. She was looking for company and so was I – it can be lonely travelling alone. She was a few years older than I, and quite attractive. I told her about myself and that I was going to Dublin just to see what it was like. She was a hairdresser and worked in a large salon in Bond Street and was going home for a two-week holiday. She had an older brother who was in the Royal Navy and was on convoy duty in the Middle East.

Knowing that I was going to look for accommodation in Dublin, she offered to ring her parents to see if they could put me up for the few days. Thus I enjoyed my first taste of the famous Irish hospitality. They lived in the Flemingstown Park area of the city and they showed me everything. I went up and down O'Connell Street, and saw the various bridges across the Liffy. I went to St Stephens Park and visited the Old Post Office, the site of the Easter Rebellion in 1916. I saw all the famous statues and went to the Abbey Theatre, I sampled draught Guinness that was like nectar and I was fed like a fighting cock as there was no rationing there. I saw my first Germans at the Embassy: it was strange seeing the Nazi swastika flying over the building. The next time I was to see that flag was when it was draped over the bodies of German soldiers of the Afrika

Corps at Medjez El Bab. They treated me right royally and would not accept a penny for it. When I arrived back in England I almost had an Irish accent.

My last leave from the Training Battalion was notable for two reasons – I met my future first wife and on my return lost my hard-earned stripes. I decided it was about time I visited my mother, who in the past months had moved again. I told her of all that had happened to me and she was very interested in my father's wife and what she and the house were like. As for my problems I was told 'that's what you get for mixing with rough Irishmen'. Two days into my leave I met the girl whom I was to marry in a few months' time; her name was Elizabeth Francis. She was a couple of years older than me, a tall dark girl with striking Celtic good looks. We got on famously together and I overstayed my leave by three days. On my return to Hobbs Barracks I got what I expected, demoted to the ranks. It was a fair swap – three days of love for two stripes. After being back a couple of weeks something happened which I had always been hoping for. Twenty guardsmen were being posted to the First Battalion and I was one of them.

The First Battalion was the cream of the regiment; most of them had seen service in Egypt pre-war and in Norway in the early days. They were the crack battalion in the Brigade of Guards, *ergo* the British Army. To top all this I was put into No. 1 Company. My dream had come to fruition; here

I was in No. 1 Company, First Battalion, Irish Guards, First British Infantry Division. I could go no higher. These new comrades of mine were something else. They were mostly aged from twenty-five upwards, all well over six feet tall. At 6ft 1in I was amongst the smallest. They were big on ability too. The drill was so smooth and effortless, one had to be a part of it to believe that such precision was possible. Their confidence and skill at arms was outstanding. They were real professionals.

It was a hard school to learn in and the discipline of the battalion was hard too, but I was proud to be of their number. I found a very close friend and comrade in Michael Dempsey, who at that time was twenty-three and came from Tullamore. Any old infantryman will tell you that to survive and lead a reasonable life as a private soldier or guardsman, one had to have a close pal. Someone to watch your kit when you were on guard or when you were on short leave, someone to see your rations were kept whilst away on some duty, to help check each other's appearance so you wouldn't get 'booked', to go to the crowded NAAFI and save a seat for you, to go out with, to share what you had with, to have fun with and to see to each other's interests. Such a pal was Michael Dempsey.

Without being over-sentimental, men can love each other. It is born of mutual suffering, hardships shared, dangers encountered, mutual experiences. It is a spiritual love and it is even stronger than brotherly love. It is called comradeship, and I have see it amongst miners, heavy steel workers, submariners and infantry soldiers.

We embarked on a series of exercises all over the country. The first of these was at Gatwick Airport. The Home Guard were defending it, we were to attack and destroy. It was great fun throwing thunderflashes and firing blanks. We went through those poor old guys like a dose of salts and had the control tower in about seven minutes. Another exercise took place on the River Dart at Dartmouth where we were to do embarking and disembarking training from assault landing craft. We looked forward to this as we were going into 'civvy' billets. Michael Dempsey and myself and four older soldiers were put in a recreation room above a local pub. On the first evening some of the lads went mad on the local 'scrumpy' which was only three pence a pint – plenty of them drank over a gallon of the stuff. During the night they woke up bursting for a leak, but the nearest WC was way across the yard at the back of the pub. The obvious happened. They whipped up a window and relieved themselves into the street below. One guy who had woken up in a drunken stupor couldn't open the window, and being unable to hold it any longer, let it go into the large fire grate. When we got up to go down to breakfast, the guy who had done it stayed behind to mop up the mess. The publican's wife served up a smashing breakfast and we were just going to tuck in when the landlord noticed water dripping onto the table. He went upstairs to check it out and came down roaring like a bull and threw us all out. He also reported us to the Sergeant Major. The six of us were marched in front of the Company Commander.

'The man who carried out this disgusting act take a pace forward,' he said. Not a sound was heard. 'Right, take them out Sergeant Major, and bring them in individually.' I was first in. 'What have you got to say about this, Kenneally?' 'I did not do it, Sir, and in any case I do not drink,' I replied. 'That is your misfortune. No one has come forward so you will be classed as guilty as the rest.' He was no mug, though. The four older soldiers were given seven extra drills and banned from the local pubs during our stay there; Dempsey and I got three drills and no ban and we all had to scrub that pub recreation room from top to bottom with disinfectant. On the Sunday we were given the day off and I took the opportunity to catch a bus to Plymouth to go and see my old friend Tipp who was stationed not far away. It was to be twelve years before we were to meet again.

We left Dartmouth for Carnforth in the Lake District, where we spent a fortnight under canvas in the most appalling conditions – it rained every day. From here we moved on to the Scottish coast where we joined the rest of the First British Infantry Division in 'Combined Operations' training. This was to comprise landings from the sea, battles in mountainous country with other troops, survival and assault course training and, naturally, plenty of route marching. We were to be based at Fort William. None of us had much enthusiasm at the prospect of spending midwinter around the foot of Ben Nevis.

As it turned out I quite enjoyed this period; it is quite an experience to march with soldiers through the swirling early-morning mists of Scottish hills. We always had a piper with us, and the only way to appreciate the pipes is in the land where they were born; one felt a touch of history and tradition as we marched along.

The platoon was to do a few days' survival training on the Isle of Mull and we sailed from Oban (well fortified with real Scotch whisky) through the Sound of Mull to land at Tobermory and move inland. It was bitterly cold and the wind got up as we sailed through the Sound. It was nearly dawn and as we turned towards Tobermory the wind turned into gale proportions. The boat tossed and bucketed about in the waves and we clung onto anything we could; we were carrying full kit and were armed to the teeth. There was much cursing. The disembarkation at Tobermory quay was most difficult and we had our first casualty. The wind was of such strength that no matter how the sailors tried, the boat would swing away from the quay and then crash into it. We had to time our jump from the boat to the quay carefully, but one poor guy did not make it and he was crushed between the boat and the sea wall. We left the boat with great respect for the Navy and thankful we were not 'Jack Tars'. Every man to his trade.

We moved into the woods, banks and braes of Mull where

we were to be self-supporting for five days. It was very cold and we built bivouacs for shelter. There was plenty of brush wood and we lit fires to dry ourselves out – my scouting days came in very handy. Mull had not been fished or the deer culled for some time. The big land owners were all away doing their bit for the war effort. Our way of fishing was hardly sophisticated. A well-placed grenade in the stream did the trick. Up would come the trout, white belly showing. There is nothing so succulent as a trout packed in clay and baked in a wood fire. We were also allowed to shoot the odd buck, and what with the wild potatoes we rooted for, plus the trout and the venison, we certainly lived it up. 'Survival' training indeed! All we needed was a few bottles of port and a bevy of serving wenches and life would have been sublime.

Nothing lasts for ever in the army and the whole battalion moved onto Ayr racecourse where we occupied the stands, stables and outbuildings. Coinciding with our arrival at Ayr was the arrival of a new commanding officer, Sergeant-Colonel C. A. Montague-Douglas-Scott. Discipline tightened up dramatically and drills were increased as if we were going to do a tour of public duties. In a way this was true. We were to be inspected by His Majesty King George VI, who was to spend most of a day with us. The big day arrived and we were lucky: it was fine and sunny. We gave the Royal Salute when the King arrived. He did not give us the usual cursory inspection. He stopped and spoke to many of the older soldiers, especially those wearing the odd medal ribbon. We executed many drill manoeuvres and the King took the salute as we marched past in quick and slow time to the Regimental tunes played by the full band. It was a good parade.

His Majesty had lunch with the officers and in the afternoon, on the racecourse proper, he inspected the men doing weapon and tactical training. My small part in this, together with the rest of the platoon, was to simulate a night patrol. The idea was to creep along in an inverted 'V' formation with the platoon commander at the head. As we practised this on the uneven ground we would occasionally stumble and fall out of line with the man we were creeping behind. Guards officers have a fetish about straight lines and to facilitate this the Tactical Training officer instructed us to hold each other's bayonet scabbard as we crept along. We felt stupid and giggled amongst ourselves as we carried the order out.

The King with his escort of officers observed our performance, which the adjutant stopped mid-way through. It was rumoured later that the King had said: 'Stop those Guardsmen creeping about. They look bloody ridiculous.' He was right. All in all it was a successful day and we received the message that His Majesty was impressed with the Regiment and wished us well.

A few days after the King's visit the powers-that-be introduced the infamous army biscuit at breakfast time in place of bread. It was about three inches square, very hard, and one had to have good teeth to crack it. Following the usual routine the Orderly officer, accompanied by the Master Cook and Colour sergeants, called for order and shouted, 'Any complaints?' There was a deathly silence for a few moments, then from the back of the hall some wag went 'Woof Woof'. There was instantaneous laughter and we all took it up – the noise of barking was deafening. Uproar ensued and it was only the arrival of the RSM and the Drill sergeants that quietened us; we were having fun. We never had biscuits again.

On our last exercise at Ayr – a night attack on a hill – a large truck from an outside unit ploughed into the rear of a marching rifle platoon and quite a number were killed and injured.

Shortly afterwards, our period of training was finished. In all honesty no battalion of infantry were better trained; we were as fit as they could possibly make us and, as the army saying goes, 'we knew our kit'. The rest was up to us.

A couple of days before we were going on embarkation leave, my Company Sergeant Major buttonholed me: 'There's a vacancy for a Lance Corporal in your platoon,' he said, 'and you are it.' I told him that I did not want it and that it was hard enough looking after myself in that lot without extra responsibility. He would brook no argument and as he was no man to cross, especially at this stage of the proceedings, I was marched in and duly promoted. During my leave I married Elizabeth Francis by special licence. A lot of young men of the regiment married their sweethearts during their embarkation leave.

CHAPTER 5

ASSAULT ON THE 'BOU'

The Battalion embarked on the P&O troopship *Strathmore*, and in convoy with eight other ships which carried the remainder of the 1st Infantry Division, we sailed down the Clyde. It was to be a most uncomfortable trip. We had to sleep in hammocks which were made for men about 5ft 8in tall, when most of the Guardsmen were 6ft and over. In all my travels with the Brigade the people who looked after the logistics of these things never took this into account, so we were always short of room. Once our convoy was well under way, the Commanding Officer told us of our future. We were going to North Africa to reinforce the 1st Army which had recently landed there. The 1st Army comprised a British Infantry Division, American and Free French Forces plus ancillary units.

The journey by sea to Africa was surprisingly uneventful. During the voyage we did endless lifeboat drill, and the Bren gunners, of which I was one, were issued with tripods and allotted various anti-aircraft positions. U-Boats were plundering the Mediterranean, but fortunately our convoy was not attacked.

My first view of North Africa was breathtaking. We approached Algiers in the late afternoon and the brilliant white colonial houses, set in terraces high above the port, contrasted vividly with the red earth of the land. It looked beautiful and peaceful. It did not seem possible that war and mayhem were going on there. I had never been out of the British Isles before and here I was in Africa.

Disillusionment soon came. We were marched to a staging camp a few miles from the port. On the way the column was strafed by a couple of German aircraft. We dived into nearby orange groves and luckily there were no casualties. We arrived at the so-called camp, then it poured with rain for three whole days. The camp turned into a sea of mud. I had camped in muddy conditions but had experienced nothing like this. It was well over ankle deep – a thick reddish slime which stuck to everything. After three days our misery ended; Part One orders stated the battalion would proceed by sea to Bône (a journey of some 400 miles) and on to a transit camp which was not all that far from the battle area. There was a terse memo from the Commanding Officer at the end of those orders, the gist of which was 'we are Guardsmen, and all clothing and equipment will be in good order for the march back into Algiers'. It took some doing, but after hours of scraping, brushing and polishing, our turnout was reasonable and we marched aboard the *Ulsterman* in good order and good heart. It was 13th March 1943.

This trip was not so uneventful, and as we sailed round the Tunisian coast we were attacked by several German aircraft, some of them carrying torpedoes. I was in the stern and managed to get off three magazines at them with the Bren. I saw the white trail of a torpedo snake by the stern of the ship – it missed by fifty feet, a close-run thing. It was only a brief action but enough to get the adrenalin pumping. I quite enjoyed it.

At Bône we did a day's drill in preparation for a St Patrick's Day parade on 17th March. This is a big day for the Irish Guards and is always celebrated, no matter where the regiment finds itself. The great day was warm and sunny. We formed up and each man received a small piece of shamrock which had been flown out by General Alexander, who was the overall commander of both the 1st and 8th Armies. With the shamrock had come a message from the General (who was an Irish Guardsman himself): 'Welcome to the Micks. Now we will get cracking.' We marched past the Transit Camp Commander with the battalion pipes and drums in full flow, watched by a large contingent of American troops with whom we became very pally afterwards. After the parade we were allowed the rest of the day off.

Most of us headed like excited schoolboys for the port of Bône to see what delights it had to offer. Michael and I palled up with a couple of GIs who knew their way around. Within three hours the town was in uproar. The lads had been drinking the local wine as if it were the ale they were used to. The results were dramatic: fights broke out, windows were smashed and soon the Military Police were dragging soldiers away. It turned out to be quite a night in the best Irish tradition. It was the last St Patrick's Day most of the battalion were ever going to see.

Next morning, we were roused early. We were going into the line at Béja, where the situation was critical. This was it, we were going into action. Halfway to Béja, a large staff car came thundering past us, full of red-tabbed staff officers who stopped the CO at the head of the convoy. Word passed down the line. Change of plan. The position of Medjez El Bab was even more critical. It was here that the Irish Guards were to play their part in the various actions that would culminate in the fall of Tunis and the collapse of the German forces in North Africa.

We moved into the Medjerda Valley (immediately renamed 'Happy Valley' by the lads) and took a line almost opposite a long, evil-looking ridge known later as 'Recce Ridge', behind which were the main German positions. The forward slopes of the ridge were covered in fixed lines by heavy machine guns from flank to flank, and the lower slopes were festooned with mines. The Germans had a pretty impregnable position here and they knew it.

Patrol activity was the order of the day. The Bren-gunners would go forward and cover the ridges and crests by day and at dusk the rifle companies would join us to prevent enemy patrols slipping through the lines at night. There was sporadic shelling by both sides during the day and we soon learnt the 'crack and thump' principle; by listening hard we knew when to take cover and when to ignore.

At night there was more activity: parachute flares from the mortars would illuminate the area, occasionally the Germans would sweep the slopes with heavy machine-gun fire and sometimes they would explode their own mines. A piece of shrapnel took the heel off Michael Dempsey's boot; otherwise nothing untoward happened.

It was the lull before the storm. The rains were over and the days were becoming hot and sunny, the nights clear and moonlit. It was the time for action. Our No 2 Company (103 officers and men) were ordered to do a probing attack on Recce Ridge. This meant advancing across the valley in the dark, climbing the mined slopes, a quick in-and-out battle on the ridge and then a withdrawal in daylight back across the valley. It looked a sticky job. Suicidal, even. We had 'stood to' at dusk, and at midnight we watched silently as No 2 Company moved out. The night was clear and we could see the stars but there was little moonlight. We watched and listened intently. Everything was unusually quiet, except for the occasional illuminating flare that went up, but that was quite normal. Just before 5am the silence was shattered by our own artillery behind us opening up. They laid a heavy barrage on the top of Recce Ridge. The noise was ear splitting and it lasted for about fifteen minutes. When the barrage ended we could hear heavy machine-gun fire and the thumping of grenades. Firing became intermittent and the artillery put down smoke, presumably to cover the Company's retreat back down the slopes. After the smoke we heard light automatic fire and occasional rifle shots, then nothing. It was daylight now. We watched and waited for No 2 Company to reappear, but they never did. Out of 103, five wounded guardsmen were the only ones to return.

As ordinary infantry soldiers, by the very nature of things, we were not privy to the 'Grand Design'. We had to do as ordered and follow the man in front — very much a case of 'Ours not to reason why, etc'. I suspect our battalion officers were in a similar position, but the powers-that-be threw No 2 Company's lives away. As was said in the First World War, 'It was not the Germans who took our lives, it was our own Generals who did for us.' Later, Recce Ridge was captured by a full battalion of the 78th Division supported by Churchill tanks. No 2 Company was completely replaced by first line reinforcements from the camp in Algiers. These new arrivals were very relieved to find anything left of the 1st Battalion — there had been persistent rumours in the rear echelons that most of the battalion had been wiped out. It was a grim-faced battalion that moved out of 'Happy Valley' (a misnomer if ever there was one).

We had all lost friends and comrades in No 2 Company and we had a score to settle. No 1 Company had a new commander, Captain Oliver Chesterton, who took over from Major Eugster. Very succinctly he gave us our battle orders and told us what he knew: it would appear that after being cleared off Recce Ridge by the 78th Division, the Germans had retreated to defensive positions on a line of hills beyond Medjez. Our tanks had tried to break through these hills into the plain beyond and so on to Tunis. This had proved impossible because of the hilly and rocky terrain. The area had been reinforced by the Herman Goering Division who were veterans of Stalingrad. They had brought with them 88mm artillery, heavy mortars and anti-tank guns. It was vital that these hills be taken out. It was an infantry job and the 1st Scots Guards, 5th Grenadiers and 1st Irish Guards were to do it. *WRONG!*

We moved out at night. It was 23rd April, Good Friday, and an eerie experience as we moved in single file across the minefields through which the engineers had cleared paths marked with thick white tape. Stealth was of the essence and the only sounds heard were the creak of equipment and the muffled curses as someone stumbled on the rocky ground. At regular intervals illuminating flares went up from the German defences. We would hit the ground and wait. Quiet voices could be heard on the radio, 'Sunray 1 to Sunray 2, everything O.K.' Chesterton was doing his stuff.

The white tapes suddenly stopped and we advanced in open order; we were on our own now. All at once fire broke out on our left and right flanks. Nothing opened up in front of us and we pressed on. Point 151, our first objective, was taken without firing a shot. Just before dawn the battalion moved out to take the next objective, Point 187. The enemy on the *Bou* beyond must have observed movement and started shelling with their heavy guns, but they were way out of range and caused us no hassle. On the way we passed the remnants of a company of Scots Guards who had been in action on our left flank. They had been relieved and were heading for a rest area. We exchanged banter with them as only soldiers can. Their Company Commander, Lord Lyell, had been killed in action. He was later to be awarded a posthumous Victoria Cross. They were in good order considering the fight they had been in and many had picked up souvenirs of the battle: Luger pistols, Nazi forage caps, binoculars, etc. Those Guardsmen gave us confidence. They had been there, they had fought and they had come back.

We moved on towards 187 and the shellfire increased. Amongst it we could hear the crack of 88mms. Whereas the heavy guns had been firing long, the 88s were firing short and we suffered little. Our biggest bugbear was the stones and rocks – when a shell exploded on the hard barren ground it threw up slivers of rock and so increased the fire power of a shell four-fold. Indeed, a piece of rock hit Micky Dempsey's steel helmet and put a dent in it the size of your fist. He was very proud of that and showed all the guys. The Germans did not fancy us and they left Point 187 in a hurry: we had taken our objective. Although overlooked by the *Bou* just over a mile away, the reverse slope of 187 was not too bad – it had some vegetation and a few shattered trees. We were ordered to dig in and prepare for a possible counter-attack. The guys started to scratch themselves hollows in the ground. Leaving Dempsey to it, I did my usual forage around to see what was going. I found a half-concealed weapon pit dug with the usual German efficiency – there were even a couple of tatty blankets, a bottle and a half of white wine, some pieces of stale brown bread, machine-gun belts and bits of equipment. I found Mick busily hacking away with his entrenching tool. 'Stop that bloody silly caper,' I said, 'and come with me.' We spent our last night together under the African stars, chewing the brown bread and toasting the previous tenants in Tunisian wine. It was Easter Sunday, 25th April 1943.

At dawn the Platoon Sergeants dug the men out of their various nooks and crannies amid much cursing and muttering. I had a bit of a sore head from the wine. We stood to and no attack came. The enemy, like us, were licking their wounds and preparing for the next attack which they knew, as we did, was sure to come. During the early morning all officers were called to an 'O' Group at Battalion HQ. The cooks prepared breakfast. We were ordered to check our equipment, clean all weapons, draw extra ammunition and grenades and fill our water bottles. We did this meticulously; every infantryman knows that his survival depends on the tools of his trade.

Some of the men settled down to write their last letters

home. I did not get the opportunity, but I probably wouldn't have written anyway, even if I had the chance – I was never a great letter writer. Captain Chesterton returned from the 'O' Group, called the company round him and gave us our orders. We would attack the *Bou* at dusk. The artillery would put down a heavy barrage, and the battalion would advance behind it. Nos 3 and 4 Companies would take Point 214 to the left of the *Bou*; HQ Company and No 2 the centre; my own company, No 1, would attack Point 212 on the right and Support Company, with the carriers, heavy machine guns and the 3" mortars, would follow up behind. It was vital that the Germans were driven off the *Bou* and that we held on to it. Without it the enemy could not control the valley or the plains beyond. Our tanks were ready and waiting if we were successful – and he emphasised we must be. They could roll on through and head for Tunis and victory would then be assured.

That was it. Very dryly he added that the cooks were preparing a slap-up dinner for us. A mass would be said for Roman Catholics and a service held for Anglicans. Those of Jewish, Buddhist or whatever other faiths, and non-believers (of which I was one), would have to do without. As an after-thought, he added that we would have to cross a cornfield which stretched for nearly a mile. We were bound to have casualties and if we passed a dead or wounded soldier we were to mark the spot with his rifle and bayonet and put his steel helmet on top. The corn was high and he did not want the following tanks to crush them into the ground. He wished us well and trusted that we would not let him or the Irish Guards down. We returned to our slit trenches in a sober mood and there was still occasional shelling.

The company runner came looking for me. 'Captain Chesterton wants to see you right away,' he said.

'Ah, Kenneally, I have a job for you. I want you to crawl over the ridge of the hill, find yourself some cover and observe the enemy. You are bound to see movement. If you think they are forming up for an attack, get on the radio quickly and I will come and join you. Take Guardsman May with you.' (May was the radio man.) He gave me his binoculars. I was pleased he had chosen me for this job as I hated skulking in the slit trenches. I felt claustrophobic in them and did not enjoy having time to think and brood. I was ever one to jump my fences as I came to them – sod thinking about it. May was not too keen on the job. He was a big guy, about 6ft 6in – you had to be to cart those heavy World War II radio sets about. We crawled over the ridge onto the forward slope looking for cover. All the time he moaned about the army, about being a radio man, the war, and Guards officers in particular. He was a typical infantry soldier, but a good one and he did his job well. We were lucky and found plenty of slitters and dug-outs. We chose a good deep one and observed what was going on.

Chesterton had given me the opportunity to see the whole

picture. Few of the guardsmen or NCOs had this chance. In army parlance I could 'appreciate the situation'.

In front of us lay a deep valley. On the other side of this were the long slopes leading up to the *Bou*, and the high points of 212 and 214 were just visible in the heat haze. To the right of 212 was a large grove of olive trees and to the right of these were the rolling plains that led towards Tunis. To our immediate right, Point 198, was another large olive grove. Joining these olive groves were fields of high waving corn which stretched for a mile or more. This was to be our line of advance, crossing the cornfield, making for the cover of the olive grove and then bearing left and up the slopes of 212 and 214. If the General in charge of operations had been standing next to me in the OP, I wonder if he would have taken the same course? It was getting very hot now and I reminded myself to top up my water bottle before the attack that night. At the bottom of the *Bou* I could make out the gun emplacements and occasionally the sun would glint on the barrels: there seemed plenty of them. To the right of Point 214 I saw two tanks crawling round the slope. There was very little activity on the *Bou* itself: the enemy infantry were taking it easy like ourselves.

Around 11am we began to get restless. We were supposed to have been relieved after two hours. The German gunners started to hammer the forward slope and the ridge between us with 88mm and heavy mortars. I spotted the puffs of smoke coming from the emplacements at the foot of the

Bou. We both cowered at the bottom of the weapon pit, taking a sneaky look now and again to see if there was any infantry follow-up. Thankfully there was none. At times we were showered with stones and rocks from the explosions. One mortar bomb had failed to explode and was stuck in the earth and stones on the rim of our pit. It sat there, still smoking with green and yellow painted bands round it, resembling a large sinister pineapple.

The shelling eased off and we looked round carefully. We had made a bad error – when the shelling had started we had naturally ducked for cover and left the radio behind us on the rim at the back of the pit. It was still there, but with a lump of 88mm shell sticking out of it. 'That's it,' I said. 'The radio's wrecked and we've been here long enough. Let's bale out.' May, not unnaturally, was in full agreement. We gathered our kit together and started to clamber out. 'Hold it,' said May. 'Look to your left.'

About 600 yards away to our left was a white painted colonial house with a large water tower behind it. I got the glasses and studied it carefully. A man had come out wearing a dirty white apron – he was a German army cook. He started stirring a big dixie that was on a stove. 'I am going to have a go at that bastard before we leave,' I said. I set up the Bren, put it on single shot and set the sights on maximum, 800 yards. I judged it to be about 600. It was a long shot and at that distance it was easy to make an error. May took the glasses to see what happened. I aimed very carefully at the distant white blob of his apron and squeezed off two shots. 'You've got him,' May shouted excitedly. 'There goes their fucking stew.' We scuttled up the hill like greyhounds out of the trap, giggling like schoolboys at having spoiled the Krauts' lunch.

I reported back to my Platoon Sergeant and May to Company HQ to report the loss of his radio. Captain Chesterton had gone to Battalion HQ with the platoon commanders for a final briefing, so I could not report to him. The cooks came round serving dixies of hot sizzling bacon and beans. There was fresh white bread and lashings of hot sweet tea. Each man was given a large orange for 'afters'. I'd eaten enough and I put mine in my small pack to eat later. Dempsey and I settled down in our weapon pit for an afternoon's kip. There was still sporadic shelling, but we were very secure. The attack on the *Bou* was not due until dusk and we would have plenty of time to sort ourselves out. Some of the men attended mass and various services organised by the Padres. We were rudely interrupted from our slumbers just after 3pm by the platoon commander and platoon sergeant. 'Out of it, on your feet, get your kit and weapons and gather round.' Lieutenant Eugster told us that at the 'O' Group they had received orders from Brigade HQ that we were to go in at 4pm instead of at dusk. Jesus Christ, I thought, this means broad daylight and I knew it was stinking hot since I'd had the doubtful privilege of seeing what was waiting for us. The general who issued these orders ought to be shot, I thought. Better still, he should come with us. The four rifle companies formed up under the lee of the hill. At zero hour, 4pm, with No 3 Company leading, we moved out into the open, walking quickly. There was about 200 yards to go to the cornfields.

Before No 3 Company reached them, the German guns opened up. Heavy guns, mortars, 88s and the devilish six-barrelled mortars plagued us. It seemed that all the artillery in the German army was having a go. As we entered the cornfield, the fire seemed to intensify. We plodded on grimly, our eyes fixed on Captain Chesterton and Lieutenant Eugster, who were leading. I was dazed and shocked: the noise was devastating; the hot blasts from explosions were scorching my face; patches of corn were burning fiercely; stones and earth thrown up by shell bursts were rattling down on my steel helmet; machine gun bursts were scything down the corn like a reaper and down with the corn went officers and men alike. It was a bloody massacre. Bullets were hissing around and you could see large pieces of shrapnel flying through the air. Unexploded rockets from the six-barrelled mortars would cartwheel across the ground, smoking like long torpedoes.

Rifle butts appeared everywhere marking the dead, dying and wounded. I stopped by one poor guardsman who was calling for water. He had shocking wounds. I could see the shattered bones of his arm and he had a gaping wound in his side. I reached for my water bottle and cursed; I had forgotten to fill it in the panic of our early start. His own water bottle was empty, riddled with shrapnel holes. I gave him all I had left and stuck his rifle in the ground beside him; he would not live long. Cursing myself for my stupidity I moved on. My mouth was very dry and choked with dust. Added to this was the searing heat of the sun. I thought that if the Germans didn't get me, thirst would. I remembered the orange in my pack and sucked that.

I caught up with Dempsey who was plodding on grimly. I looked to my right and left. The line of guardsmen was very thin indeed. In front of us Captain Chesterton was hit and went down. This is it, I thought. He struggled to his feet with the help of his servant who had never been far from him. We made it to the last olive grove, where we hoped to find some cover. There was plenty. This had been the site of the six-barrelled mortars, the same that I had observed from Point 187. The Germans had retreated in a hurry and left three of them. There were ammunition boxes everywhere, ration cases, equipment of all sorts — even a water carrier. We hastily filled our water bottles and I held my head under the tap. This did me a world of good and I felt better.

The enemy had realised that some of us had made this haven and pounded us with heavy fire. We dived into the long, well-made trenches and dug-outs for cover. The shelling was very accurate: it must have been a well-registered target. We sustained more casualties. After about twenty minutes (it seemed like twenty years) the shelling eased off. Four of us had taken shelter in this particular bunker and one of the guys heard German voices at the end of it. We crept along and sure enough we heard them too. The end of the bunker opened out onto a purpose-built concrete emplacement with a thick wooden door and wooden latch. It must have been a store or ammunition dump. The voices came from behind it. Dempsey and another Guardsman whipped the door open and myself and the other guy threw in a grenade each. We slammed the door shut and scuttled away. The grenades were five-second timers and I counted 3–4–5. The two grenades exploded almost simultaneously, the blast blowing the door out. The smell was terrible – blood and gunpowder. I peered into the dark interior. There must have been twenty Germans scattered about in there. They were all bandaged up already and those that were not dead were screaming their heads off. This place was where the retreating enemy had left their wounded. I turned away without the slightest compassion for them. They had done much worse to my dead and wounded comrades lying out there in the burning cornfields.

Whilst our little action was going on, the Captain was gathering up the remnants of No 1 Company and No 4 Company, who had lost all their officers and senior NCOs. We were a little better off. We had the Captain, Lieutenant Eugster, and Sgt Fanning left. The orders filtered down the slit trenches and bunkers. We could rest and recover until it got half light then the company would do a sort of left wheel, advance in open order up the slopes of 212 and 214 and take the *Bou*.

'Time gentlemen,' shouted Lieutenant Eugster and clambered out of the trench. Sullenly, and with not too much enthusiasm, we prepared to follow him. At that moment the shelling and machine guns opened up again, and we slithered back into the trenches. Seeing this, the Lieutenant jumped onto a fallen tree and shouted, 'Come on.' Within seconds, he was dead. I don't know what hit him; it could have been a machine-gun burst or shrapnel.

We followed Chesterton, who was plodding up the slopes of Point 212 with that grim determination that was fast becoming his hallmark. He went down again, hit by shrapnel. We paused for a few seconds. The sod got up again and, like a staggering boxer, he led on. I am perfectly sure that in this final phase of the attack, if he had stayed down, most of us would have hightailed it back to the safety of the trenches and bunkers we had left behind us.

It was getting towards darkness and half way up the hill the order came to fix bayonets. There was something like a company of German infantry scattered among the rocks. Some shots were exchanged, but they did not want to know and scuttled up the hill over the ridge and away. We had made it: the *Bou* was ours. The shelling stopped; the firing stopped. All that could be heard were the cries and groans of the wounded. I passed Captain Chesterton, supported by his servant, as he headed for the RAP (Regimental Aid Post) at the rear. He looked as if he needed it. His tunic was badly torn, battledress trousers sodden with blood, face black with powder burns and his arm was hanging badly. 'Ah, Kenneally,' he said. 'Are you all right?' 'I'm fine, thank you Sir,' I replied. He had done his job well, he had got us there. Nearly forty years on I met him again at Wellington Barracks for the unveiling of a statue of Field Marshal Alexander. 'Ah, Kenneally. Are you all right?' 'I'm fine, thank you Sir,' I replied.

It was pitch dark now and everything was quiet. Some of the men started digging trenches to get some cover. I looked for Dempsey in the darkness but could not find him. I was mentally and physically shattered. The Bren felt like a ton weight; I'd had enough. I looked around and found two large boulders with a hollow between them. That'd do me. I lay down in the hollow and was asleep in seconds.

CHAPTER 6

'A CALCULATED RISK'

I awoke with the hot sun on my face. Good God, I thought, I had slept like a baby for eight hours. I felt completely refreshed and cast my mind back to the previous day's proceedings. Forget it, I said to myself, and wiped my mind clear. This is another day, another dollar.

I scrambled to my feet and took stock of the situation. The high ridge of the *Bou* stretched some 1500 yards between Points 212 and 214. It consisted mainly of solid rock for about 25 yards each side of the slope. It then tapered down into barren scrub. There was a road halfway down Point 212 that led down into the Gab-Gab Gap. It was not a place of great beauty. In the centre of the ridge, just below the crest, was what looked like a German observation bunker. Each side of the bunker small groups of guardsmen were digging in and moving large rocks to give themselves cover. This did not look good to me. They must be expecting attacks from either side of the hill. This meant only one thing: we were not far off from being surrounded by the enemy.

At this point it might be wise to quote from the Official War Diary: 'On that morning, 27th April, 173 guardsmen armed only with Brens, rifles and grenades held the hill.

On Friday night, 30th April, after five large attacks, 80 Irish Guardsmen still held it.' Of those 173 survivors of the cornfields there were only five officers, no warrant officers and only one senior NCO.

I found the remnants of No 1 Company at the right of the line. There was only one NCO left, Lance Sergeant 'Liz' Fanning and seventeen guardsmen. 'Liz' was a pre-war regular and probably the smartest soldier in the regiment. He was a strange character and not much liked by the officers and warrant officers. He was a bit of a 'chancer', added to which he was a barrack-room lawyer and never did any more than he had to, but he was shrewd, intelligent and above all a great survivor. Most of the guardsmen left were old regulars – Lavery, the Brigade's Light Heavyweight Champion, 'Hopper' Adamson, a tough Geordie and as hard as nails, Cafferty, the biggest rogue in the regiment, Old 'Grey Wolf' Brogan, so called because of his prematurely grey hair, a very quiet man but an ace soldier. There was Ross, 'the mule man', and a few others like them. The remainder of the Company was made up of younger soldiers like myself and Dempsey.

'I wondered what had happened to you,' said Liz. 'I thought you were a goner. I sent Dempsey to look for you.' It transpired that Mick had found me but, as I was fast asleep, he told Liz he had looked around and had not been able to find me. 'No matter,' Liz said. 'You are now second in command of the Company.' (A doubtful honour, I thought.) 'The carriers have gone up as far as they can and have dumped some supplies. Take four men and see what you can find. We need ammo, food and water.' There was no lack of volunteers for this detail. It was getting very hot and we were all thirsty and hungry. In the end I took six of them. As we walked out down the hill, the ravages of the previous day's battle lay all around us; arms and equipment everywhere. The bodies of both British and German soldiers were scattered about, flies swarming over their open wounds, and in the oppressive heat the smell of corrupted flesh and death was horrible. The wounded had obviously been taken away, but the dead would have to wait.

We found no dumps, but further down one of the guys spotted a carrier lying on its side; it had obviously hit a mine. One track had been blown off and I warned the men to tread carefully. We got lucky. We found a sack of bread and some large tins of bully beef. There was no water, but there were a couple of canisters of cold tea and boxes of .303 ammunition. In an abandoned 'Recce Regiment' armoured car we found a jerry can half full of water. There were also two land mines. 'We'll take those as well,' I said, 'they might come in handy.' We struggled back up to the ridge with our booty and handed it all over to Liz who, apart from being commanding officer, appointed himself quartermaster as well. He doled out half a mug of cold tea, a lump of bread and a slice of bully to each of us. He was very sparing with it. Just as well, since that food and water was all we were going to get for three full days and we had to share it with others. Our position on the hill had deteriorated. Because of the high slopes our support company had been unable to bring up the 3in mortars, anti-tank and Vickers machine guns and, most importantly, the No 19 wireless set; our only link with Brigade HQ and the outside world was stranded at the bottom of the *Bou*.

For this reason, the commanding officer left a small HQ on the hill with the Adjutant, Captain Fitzgerald, in charge. The CO left for hill 187 on the other side of the Gab-Gab Gap and set up his main HQ there. It was fortunate he left when he did. Soon afterwards German tanks and infantry moved into the Gap and took over. We were out on a limb and virtually surrounded. We were joined by a Sergeant Salt and two privates of the Reconnaissance Regiment who had been left stranded on the *Bou* when the Germans closed it off.

About noon, the enemy started to mortar the ridge heavily but we were well dug in and it was bearable. Two hours later they really opened up with 88mms and heavy HE from tanks. This was from close range. They were firing at us from the olive groves. This fire was very vicious and accurate and we started to get casualties. It forced us to evacuate that side of the ridge and occupy the trenches we had dug the other side. They were really softening us up. At 1500 hours the fire intensified with salvo after salvo of six-barrelled mortars screaming at us. The expected happened;

we heard rifle and Bren-gun fire on our left flank. The German Infantry were attacking the remnants of 3 and 4 Companies on Point 214. The shelling slackened off and the rifle and Bren fire increased. We were not engaged.

A runner came over from Point 214 asking if we could help them out. Myself and nine guardsmen, roughly half of No 1 Company, ran over and flopped down beside the guys from Nos 3 and 4. They were holding them all right. I estimated there were over a hundred German infantry about 50 yards in front of us. They were scattered amongst the rocks firing rifles and semi-automatics; the nearest of them were chucking stick grenades. Those are the guys for me, I thought. I put the Bren on single shot: at this range a man could not miss. I downed quite a few and the increased fire power had its effect as one or two of them started to retreat. Soon it was a general flight and we picked them off as they retreated into the cornfield below. It gave us a great lift and I felt quite elated. It had been the closest we had ever been to our German counterparts and we had beaten them. Soldiers being what they are, the 100 enemy had grown to 500 by the time we rejoined our comrades on 212. No matter, the odds had been at least three to one in their favour and we had proved a point.

After an hour, the shelling and mortaring started again. We suffered more casualties; the dead we left where they were after removing their AB64s and identity discs; the badly wounded we carried to the bunker where the Adjutant looked after them. The walking wounded had to make their way down the western slopes to Gab-Gab Gap where there was a Regimental Aid Post. Some of them ran into German patrols and never made it. The worst hardship was thirst. We had no protection from the blazing African sun and the air was thick with rock dust from the exploding shells.

Towards dusk the shelling increased and we all knew what that meant. As it darkened and the shelling eased we could hear them: guttural German commands, the noise of their heavy boots on the rocks, the muffled grunts and curses as they hauled themselves over the terrain. The noise started to recede and we wondered where they were going to hit us from. We soon knew. They attacked 214 again and despite fierce resistance the men of 3 and 4 Company were overrun and the Germans flooded over the top and made along the ridge heading towards us on 212. We were well and truly in the manure business. We had a stroke of luck, however. Previously, under cover of half light, Sergeant Musgrove of the 3" mortar platoon had managed to bring up an unassembled mortar and twenty bombs from the foot of the *Bou* — no mean feat in itself. As the attack started, he quickly assembled the mortar and blasted off at the Germans coming over the top at 214. It stopped them dead in their tracks. He fired off all twenty bombs. They never imagined we had such fire power and they retreated helter-skelter with 3 and 4 Companies in full cry after them. This left the German infantry, who had come over the top, trapped in the centre.

94

It was dark now and chaos ensued. They ran in all directions looking for an avenue of escape. This was no time for niceties and I hose-piped those I could see with the Bren. The riflemen chucked grenades at them and we soon finished them off. All firing stopped and in the unusual quietness we heard them digging in at the bottom of the hill. They would reinforce and be back at us tomorrow. It was obvious they wanted us off the *Bou*.

In the half light of dawn we stood to again, but happily all was quiet. They were to attack later. I had noticed that Michael Dempsey was not there and when we stood down I went to look for him. I found him and was knocked sick. He was dead and had been for some hours; so was the young 'Recce' Private who was in the slit trench with him. They had received a direct hit from an HE shell in the previous night's heavy barrage. Their wounds were horrific and both must have died instantly.

As I cut Mick's AB64 out of his back pocket I shivered with the cold. The sun had not yet come up and I pulled the German greatcoat I was wearing around me. Some of us had picked these up from our dead protagonists and they were very useful in the cold nights. I walked back slowly and thought about him. It was not really his war – he had no loyalty to King and country or the British Empire. Like so many Southern Irish men he had joined the British army looking for fun and adventure. The only duty he owed was to the five-pointed star that we were all proud to wear. He had carried that duty out. A true mercenary was Michael Dempsey, one of Kipling's 'Wild Geese'.

I was in a very morose mood as I gave Mick's AB64 to Liz Fanning. 'Have a drink of this, Johno,' he said. I looked at him – it was the first time he had ever called me that. He knew Mick and I had been muckers and I felt that he and the tough old regulars around him had accepted me as one of them – I had won my spurs. It was raw Cognac and made me cough. 'Where did you get this?' He jerked his thumb at the dead enemy from the previous night's work. 'Go and help yourself.'

I walked amongst them. There was one youngster all curled up in a ball. He looked about seventeen and it appeared that he had died the same way as he had come into this world, all curled up in his mother's womb. Nearby lay a very different type, a grey-haired Feldwebel whose teeth were bared in a grimace. He had died hard. He wore the ribbon of the Iron Cross on his tunic. He looked a tough cookie. I thought, 'I bet he's got drink on him,' and unhooked his water bottle – it contained wine.

It struck me forcibly as I wandered amongst them that these guys were just the same as us; they suffered as we suffered, they died as we died or were going to die and the only difference between us was our uniforms. I respected them.

I noticed a slight movement of a body to my right. 'Christ,' I thought, 'one of them's alive.' I turned him over warily with my foot. He looked at me with stark terror in his eyes as he thought I was going to shoot him. There was no danger of that; I was sick of the killing. I looked at him. Both of his legs were shattered where he had received a machine-gun burst across them. He struggled onto his elbows, reached into his tunic and handed me some photographs. 'Meine Frau, Meine Frau,' he said. They were pictures of a young woman with a child. 'Alright son,' I said, 'with a bit of luck and a following wind you'll see them again.' I called over two guardsmen and we carried him over to Battalion HQ and handed him over to Captain Fitzgerald. 'He'll have to take his chance outside. There is no room at the inn.' He was right. The bunker was packed with the wounded. The Captain was doing a great job. Strangely enough, I was to see that German soldier again.

As we walked back to our positions, a captain and five guardsmen came up the hill. These must be the rumoured reinforcements – five, when we could have done with five hundred. The officer called me over and asked me where Captain Fitzgerald and Battalion HQ were. I pointed the way and to my surprise he got a 'move' on me. 'Take that German greatcoat off, Corporal, it sets a bad example to the men.' I looked at him and was about to tell him where to go. Discipline prevailed: you don't argue with Guards officers. I took it off.

I rejoined Liz Fanning and the others just as he was doling out the rations. There were about fourteen of No 1 Company remaining. Around 9.00am the shelling and mortaring started again. Our lookout man on the forward slope shouted that there was movement way down below. Liz said, 'You had better go and have a look and send him back up, he's been out there from stand-to and he's had no grub. Do you want a No 2?' I slid over the ridge and took over the OP. The guy was right. There was movement, plenty of it, and it looked as if the target was going to be our positions on Point 212.

Trucks and armoured vehicles were disgorging infantry at the bottom of the lower slope. The sun was up now and their steel helmets glistened. One thing, I thought, was that they were not seasoned troops as no self-respecting infantry would climb the hill in bunches as they were doing. They must be reinforcements from Tunis which was only fourteen miles away.

The shelling increased. It seemed as if they were trying to knock the top off the ridge behind me. The lads must be having it rough. I ducked lower myself as I was being showered by rocks and rubble. When the barrage eased, I took another look.

I could not see them but I could hear them. There were two large boulders about ten yards in front of me so I ran to them and took cover. A German voice was very clear now. I left the Bren gun behind the boulders and crawled through the scrub. The ground fell away into a deep gully and there they were. Most of them were squatting round a

German officer. Some were lying down taking a breather and they were bunched like a herd of cattle. What an opportunity. I crawled back to the boulders and quickly took off all my equipment – speed was to be the essence of this operation. I put a new magazine on the Bren gun and one in each pocket. 'Here goes,' I said to myself. I took a deep breath and belted forward, firing from the hip. I achieved complete surprise. I hose-piped them from the top of the gully. They were being bowled over like ninepins and were diving in all directions. I had time to flip on another magazine and I gave them that too. Enough was enough, and I fled back to the boulders and safety.

The remaining Germans had scattered and were firing everywhere, even at each other. Bullets were shattering off the boulder in front of me. The lads from No 1, hearing the firing, came over the top screaming like banshees and were picking them off left, right and centre. They fled down the hill and out of sight. 'Holy Mother of Christ,' Liz Fanning said, as he viewed the carnage below. 'What have you done?'

'Nothing to it,' I replied, as I picked up my equipment and went for a drink of his cognac.

It was to be a busy day. We had only rested for twenty minutes when another attack started in the centre of the *Bou* a few yards below the bunker. No 4 Company were dealing with it capably and we gave them a hand. One of our guys, 'Mule Man' Ross, so called because he looked after the mules in Egypt, received what we call a 'through and through' in the face. He was a big stolid man with the unfortunate habit of always having his mouth open, which not unnaturally gave him a rather gormless look. A bullet had gone through one cheek and out of the other; if he had had his mouth shut the bullet would have shattered his jaw and done untold damage – perhaps Guardsman Ross was not so gormless after all. In fact the two round scars he carried earned him many pints when it was all over – he was very proud of them.

Later that morning Liz sent me with three men down the hill to see if any supplies had been dumped the previous night. We had no water left, no food, and ammunition was getting short. We were living off what we could find. Halfway down the hill I met CQMS Mercer who had left a carrier packed with most of what we wanted further down. He was on his way to report to the bunker. I sent my three men down to get everything they could carry and I walked back up with Mercer.

We walked slap bang into a German squad of four setting up an MG 600 machine gun. They must have infiltrated right round the hill and if we had arrived fifty seconds later they would have stitched us up good and proper. As it was, I gave them a quick burst with the Bren gun and both of us dived for cover. I knew I had stopped two of them as I had seen their arms throw up as the bullets ploughed into them. Mercer and I were at the wrong end of the stick and I realised what the Germans felt like – it ain't so easy fighting uphill. We could not have been more than 15 yards below them and they started to throw stick grenades at us. It was most uncomfortable. Mercer told me to keep pooping off with the Bren so that he could work round above them and take them out with the Sten. He managed it. We won. We formed a friendship that day that was to last for many years.

In the afternoon, with the sun at its height, the enemy tried a new tactic. From our right we could see into the plain below. Three tanks in single file were creeping up the hill, followed by infantry. You can stop men with machine guns and rifles, but not tanks. The route they were taking meant they would not have to cross the ridge and they were coming up behind us. We watched their inexorable progress up the hill. They were slipping and sliding on the rocks but were creeping nearer. Liz Fanning ordered us to gather up all our arms and ammunition and prepare to evacuate our hard-won piece of ground. We had no anti-tank guns, PIATs and no ammo for the 3" mortar. But we did have the two red mines that I had brought up a couple of days ago. No volunteer came forward to run down the hill and place a mine under the leading tank's track though: a soldier does not mind dying but who's going to commit suicide? How were we to detonate the mines?

We decided on our course of action. We tied a hand grenade with a seven-second fuse to each mine. We would wait until the leading tank got fairly near and the two biggest and strongest men, Liz Fanning and Guardsman Pollock, would pull out the pins and throw them as far as they could and we would all pray that they would roll into the tank's path and stop it. If that failed we would bale out and let them have our part of the damned hill. We watched anxiously as the two red mines went sailing through the air. One stopped where it fell, the other rolled down into the path of the tank. We ducked down and waited. There were two massive explosions and we were covered in dust and rubble. We looked out. We had not stopped the tank but we had put the fear of God up the tank commander. He must have thought an anti-tank was lining him up to blow him away. The tank skidded round and high-tailed it down the hill a lot quicker than he came up it and the two others followed suit.

Friday morning, 30th April, started relatively quiet. There was no dawn attack and the shelling and mortaring was desultory. We took stock of the situation. No 1 Company was down to ten men including Liz Fanning and myself. We had a fair amount of .303 ammo but no grenades, and I had only two magazines left for the Bren gun. We had some stale bread and a large tin of bully, but we had no water. 'Let's go and see what we can scrounge,' Liz said. 'We'll take Cafferty with us – if there is anything, he'll find it.' Cafferty was the ultimate Irish rogue. If you had nothing, Cafferty was the man to supply you with something – a good guy to have around. Liz reported to the Adjutant and told him of our position. We were down to eighty fit men, he said, but were expecting reinforcements any time – we had been expecting them for some time already. He gave us a box of grenades and one reinforcement, Sergeant Salt, the last survivor of the 'Recce troop' which had been unfortunately stranded with us on the *Bou*.

We walked along the whole ridge chatting to friends and comrades. The ridge in front of No 2 Company was pounded flat and they had very little cover. They had sustained the most casualties. No 3 and 4 companies were not much better off on Point 214 – the slope up to them was much more gentle than that of 212. Our cover was much better.

We met Sergeant Clem Gundel of No 4 who gave us half a jerry can of water. He had a bad facial wound but he was carrying on. We called him the 'Chief', because he was a top-class soldier and would always give you half of what he had. I saw Guardsman May, the radio man, who was now a rifleman with No 3. We all looked pretty rough: none of us had shaved for days, we were covered with rock dust from the heavy shelling and many were bloodstained from carrying the wounded. I could well understand the German infantry not relishing having to tangle with them – they terrified me, and I was one of them.

Morale was high, and during this lull the guys were laughing and joking and taking the mickey out of each other. The three of us moved back to our position and found the lads eating a belated breakfast. Cafferty as usual had come up trumps and they were tucking into soya link sausages and beans. I saw Sergeant Salt smile to himself. He had landed amongst a right bunch.

Around 11.00am it seemed as if the world was falling in: the enemy bombarded us with every gun they had — field guns, 88mms, tanks and six-barrelled mortars. This was to be their final attack and they tried to blast us off the *Bou*. They were following up with masses of infantry and there were many more German officers than I had ever seen before. They were attacking all round. I saw a line of tanks heading for 3 and 4 Companies on 214. There were no tanks on our flank; perhaps the previous day's effort had put them off and they thought there were anti-tank guns sited there.

Sergeant Salt and I were in the very same OP that I had occupied the day before. It was almost a re-run. The same two large boulders were in front of us and we could see the enemy advancing on the same line. There were more of them than yesterday with officers leading individual groups. We watched intently as they came toward us. I had told Salt of the success I had had yesterday and when they disappeared out of sight into the gully below us, I asked him if he wanted to have a go. 'I'm game,' he said. I had the Bren and he had a Sten gun. 'Are you ready?' 'O.K.,' he said, and we both dashed forward to the lip of the gully. They were there all right and we surprised them; we each emptied a magazine, spraying bullets all round.

These guys were of a different mettle to yesterday's outfit

and started firing at us. 'Run for it,' I shouted to Sergeant Salt and sprinted for the ridge. The Germans started clambering over the gully and tried to pick us off. No 1 Company came over the top firing rifles and throwing grenades. Bullets were hissing and spattering round my feet and out of the corner of my eye I saw poor Sergeant Salt go down with a machine gun burst in the back. As I reached the top of the ridge a great blow hit me in the right leg. It knocked me flying over the top and tumbled me into an empty slit trench. Meanwhile No 1 were beating them off: that box of grenades proved to be priceless. The enemy below us retreated and joined up with the attacks on 2, 3 and 4 Companies. Brogan ripped open my trouser leg. I had a bullet wound just under the right knee and deep into the calf. Still, I felt myself lucky. Sergeant Salt was dead. We had lost one guardsman and Pollock had been shot through the shoulder. Brogan poured sulpha-anamide powder into our wounds and applied Field Dressings. The powder was a godsend as we were all terrified of gangrene poisoning which quickly set in with the hot climate.

Meanwhile, attack after attack was going on at Point 214. Indeed, No 2 Company had been overrun by tanks and two or three of them had been taken prisoner. We were ordered to evacuate our positions and every man was to line up with 3 and 4 Companies where the fighting was at its peak. Pollock and I hobbled after them as the lads ran down the ridge. Pollock had only one usable arm but he had picked up a Luger pistol. I still had the Bren and a guardsman tried to grab it off me. I told him to 'piss off' — that gun had served me well and was going to serve me some more. We dropped down beside No 4. It was close combat stuff. The German infantry came over the rocks in droves. Grenades and stick grenades were passing each other in the air like snowballs. The air was full of the chatter of machine guns and the ground we lay on trembled with the explosions of grenades. There was no time for fear; a strange 'don't-give-a-damn' feeling took a grip — something every infantryman feels when he is constantly exposed to death in brutal and violent forms. Two German figures loomed over us and I cut one of them in half with the Bren. Pollock shot the other in the face.

Suddenly they were not round us any more. They had started to break and were firing at us as they retreated. As one man we all got up and chased after them, though we hobbled behind, and we shot into them as they fled. Those who could not run were bayoneted from behind. We cheered and shouted 'Up the Micks' as they fled — well to the fore was big Guardsman May.

And that was it. They never came again. After the battle was over, seven hundred German dead were counted around the *Bou*. I say that with no pride. Of the 1st Battalion Irish Guards, just eighty came off the hill. Out of it all we learned respect for the Germans: they did what they had to do just as we did; they stuck their faces into the same ground as we did; they were covered in the same filth and rubble as we were – after all, a shell does not care who it kills.

After the operation was over there came two messages. The Divisional Commander wrote: 'May I express my very great admiration for the gallant conduct of the 24th Guards Brigade. The 1st Division was selected to bear the brunt of forcing an entry through the crust of the enemy to enable the armour to break through. All three brigades had very strong enemy positions to attack which they did most gallantly. The relentless courage and cheerful sacrifices and the great tenacity of the 24th Guards Brigade was outstanding. And indeed, without it the victory of First Army could never have been achieved. Whilst it is impossible to differentiate between the conduct of all three battalions, I think the story of the Irish Guards on Hill 212 will always stand in red letters on the pages of that glorious Regiment's history. Your losses were great and terrible, but my heart goes out to you in thankfulness that such courage should produce a reward, the true value of which, at this time, no man can assess.'

The second message was from General Alexander. It read: 'Heartiest congratulations to you and all ranks of the battalion for your magnificent fight, which has not only added fresh laurels to the illustrious name of the regiment, but has also been of the utmost importance to our whole battle. I am immensely proud of you all. I am very sorry about your losses. A white marble cross now stands on Hill

212. It simply states: "To the memory of the Officers, Warrant Officers, Non-Commissioned Officers and Guardsmen of the 1st Bn. Irish Guards who died on and around this hill April 27th–30th, 1943. *Quis separabit?*"

Everything was quiet now; no shelling, no firing, no sounds of men digging in. Only the cries and groans of the wounded. The aftermath of a battle is a terrible experience. Once the shooting stops and the adrenalin and bloodlust goes, all that is left is to count the cost. It was getting near dusk and the order came round: 'All walking wounded report to the bunker.' That included Pollock and me and we made our way to the Adjutant. He had a quick look at my leg. The blood had all congealed but there was a nasty blue ring round the wound. 'I don't like the look of that, Kenneally,' he said. 'You'll have to make your way down to the RAP whilst it's still light.' He said the same to Pollock. 'Leave your Bren and any ammunition you have left,' he added. I dropped it on the pile without a backward glance. After all, it is only a tool. We helped each other down the hill. I noticed Bill Pollock had shoved the Luger inside his tunic; after all, it was not WD property and he could get £50 off the Yanks for it. On the way down we met a company of Gordon Highlanders coming up the hill in single file. They were being led by a white-haired Major who looked a hundred years old. He was walking with a long stick with a V-shaped cleft at the top – it looked like a shepherd's crook. He asked if he was going in the right direction to relieve the 1st Irish Guards. I told him to look for the bunker on the ridge. As we passed by the Gordons they all looked very young. I assured those who asked that it was all over. They offered us cigarettes and chocolate. I did not smoke then but I gladly accepted the chocolate.

My leg was stiffening up. It was not too painful, just an angry throb. Bill Pollock found me a long stick and we moved on down a little quicker. Strangely, we were both in a gay mood. I had noticed similar gaiety amongst the Scots Guards when we met them returning from their action on Point 145. We were gay because we were alive.

We crossed the Gab-Gab Gap and made it to the Regimental Aid Post. They gave us a good reception. Drill Sergeant Kenny shoved a mug of steaming hot sweet tea in my hand and it tasted like nectar. Cooks and orderlies asked after their pals on the *Bou*: had this guy made it, what happened to so and so — it felt like family. The Medic Sergeant replaced our wound dressings and told us we would have to go to the Casualty Clearing Station which was near Beja, about twenty-five miles away. It was dark now and the ambulances and trucks would not be coming until first light. We were given a hot meal and a couple of blankets each. I slept like a baby.

During the night more wounded had been brought in, one or two Jocks and Grenadiers and guys from line regiments amongst them. The ambulances and a three-ton truck lined with benches duly turned up. The seriously wounded were placed in the red cross ambulances and the walking wounded placed in the truck. Because I had a leg wound they placed me on a stretcher – it felt like lying on corrugated iron. As I lay waiting to be carried in I thought 'sod this', and scrambled up to join Bill in the three-tonner. I wanted to be with a 'mucker' and there was every chance we would be separated. After a bumpy ride we arrived at the CCS to be faced with a RAMC Sergeant and orderlies. 'Is there anyone seriously ill?' he bawled. 'They can come off first.' A voice from the back of the truck piped up, 'Of course not, we've come to play you at cricket.'

That sally set the mood and we baled out quite cheerfully, but it was not to last. The CCS was a hive of activity. We were directed to join a queue outside a large marquee tagged 'Walking Wounded'; the stretcher cases and seriously injured were taken to other tents and laid outside and the most serious and the dying went straight in. As we lolled about waiting our turn for treatment, a medic corporal and four privates came round dishing out tea and sandwiches, and a packet of cigarettes each or chocolate for non-smokers.

I had noticed a group of soldiers gathered to one side. They looked a disconsolate bunch but much the same as us, covered in dust, scorched clothing and unshaven. All the medics appeared to leave them alone and walked on by. I said to the medic corporal, 'What about those guys, don't they get anything?' He replied, 'We don't bother with them.

They're LMF cases.' 'LMF,' I said. 'What's that?' 'Lack of Moral Fibre,' he replied. 'They've run away from the battles and we have had orders to leave them until last.'

I looked at the corporal: his trousers still retained a crease, his shirt was pressed and he was well shaven. It was obvious that the nearest he'd been to a battle was in bed with a reluctant girlfriend. 'What the fuck do you know about it?' I said. I grabbed the tea dixie from him and limped over to them. Bill took sandwiches and others followed suit. Frightened and wild-eyed, one or two had the shakes, obviously suffering from shell shock, and could hardly drink the tea.

There was bound to be the odd malingerer amongst them, but they had all been there at the thick end, and who were those bastards to judge them? Most soldiers develop resilience, but there were some who would never acquire it. Such men were these. We were all disgusted at their treatment. Later, the powers-that-be took notice of such incidents – in future campaigns the condition was named 'Battle Fatigue' and its sufferers treated with much more compassion.

Evacuation followed swiftly and we were piled into Dakotas and flown by the Americans to the 60th General at Algiers. It was the first time I had ever been in an aircraft and it was quite a thrill. The Yanks treated us with every kindness and were very friendly. The flight was not a long one and as they unloaded the stretcher cases, lo and behold, amongst them was the German infantryman whom I had tended to on the *Bou*. I tapped him on the shoulder and stuck my thumb up. He gave me a smile as they carried him away. I don't know if he recognised me but I was glad for him – it looked as though he was going to make it.

The hospital was made up mostly of tents, with the main building for the seriously wounded. We quickly went to surgery and the bullet was removed from my calf. It was a 9mm, probably from a Schmeisser machine gun. The surgeon gave it to me but I soon lost it.

Bill and I ended up in the same ward. We were a mixed bunch from many regiments, fifteen men each side of the large tent with trestle tables down the centre with benches each side. The RAMC medics did all the hard dirty work associated with wounded soldiers. The nurses, who were mainly QAs, changed dressings, dished out pills and gave injections, all under the eagle eye of the matron who was a hardened old army nurse. She had an air of authority and a sharpness of tongue to match any Regimental Sergeant Major I had ever come across.

Discipline was very strong, and the hospital was no rest home. One evening when the night nurses trooped in to take over, someone quite jokingly shouted: 'Here come the women, chaps, let's throw them across the beds and have some fun.' The staff nurse marched the nurses out and within three minutes four MPs came in, picked up the soldier, still in his bed, and carried him off to what they called the miscreants tent. Here, the unruly ones got necessary medical attention and little else, sometimes with a period of detention afterwards, depending on their offences.

The matron need not have worried: the majority of the nurses had little time for rough soldiers and you had to have at least three pips to warrant their attention. Not all were like that, though, and one particular nurse was extremely kind and patient.

The padres and priests were well in evidence, writing letters home for those incapable of doing so, saying masses and holding services most days. They were always inviting us to pray and thank God for our deliverance. Quite a few attended these services and undoubtedly got some comfort out of them. Before the horrors of the cornfields and the *Bou* I was an unbeliever – afterwards more so. I just could not believe that it was God who guided men's destinies rather than man himself. If you turned your head one way you stopped a bullet, if you turned the other way it missed. It was pure luck if you survived. The only good things that came out of conflict were prompted by a man's own conscience and his upbringing. Nothing that has happened since has prompted me to change that point of view.

After a week my leg was much better and healing nicely. Bill Pollock had regained full use of his shoulder. After a fortnight we were near enough fit for release and preparations were being made for our return. Line regiment soldiers were to go to a large reinforcement depot at Philippeville for a period of rest and rehabilitation.

Bill and I had heard about the rest and rehabilitation at Philippeville and how it was in fact no rest but plenty of the other: six-mile runs and walks, loads of PT and bags of bullshit, or so we heard. We managed to avoid finding out. We agreed to go along with the transport to Philippeville where we would bale out and make our own way to Tunis where our battalion was resting.

We were all dropped off outside the orderly room at Philippeville and told to report in. We walked away through the camp gates and on to the Bizerta-Tunis road. There was plenty of troop transport on the road – tank transporters, guns and troop carriers aplenty. The snag was they were nearly all going to Bizerta. A brand new Royal Artillery portec truck towing a Bofors gun came trundling up and I flagged the driver down. 'Where are you heading for, chum,' I asked. 'Tunis airport,' he replied. 'Any chance of a lift?' The driver turned to the gunner sergeant sitting next to him, who looked at me and said, 'I know you, don't I?' Recognition dawned on me – he was the bombardier who with others had replaced the under 21s at Wantage when my old battery had joined the BEF in France. 'What are you doing in that crowd?' he asked, spotting my Irish Guards Flashes. 'I transferred to them,' I replied. 'Hop in,' he said, and we were on our way. It was a lucky coincidence. They had come up from Algiers and were going to stop at Bône for the night, moving on to Tunis the next day. They shared what they had with us and we talked over old times. It seemed that when the battery had been decimated in Belgium by the German Panzers he had been at the rear collecting ammunition with a fatigue party. He had joined the general retreat to the Channel ports. After being attacked by German dive-bombers they had lost their truck and marched the last seventy miles to Dunkirk. He and his party were on one of the last transports from the beach. He was posted to an Ack-Ack unit and was joining a unit at Tunis Airport. He had not remembered my name and I did not enlighten him.

Next day as we approached the outskirts of Tunis, I spotted the familiar white triangle of the 1st British Infantry Division nailed to a tree. It was Div HQ. They directed us to a place called Manouba where the 1st Irish Guards were bivouaced. The gunner sergeant drove us to the door and we were home. The lads gave us a great welcome and gathered round to hear our tales and we listened to theirs as they brought us up to date. The battalion had been relieved on the *Bou* by a company of the 5th Grenadiers at point 214 and at point 212 by the company of Gordon Highlanders that I had met toiling uphill, led by the white-haired Major. The 7th and 6th Armoured Divisions had smashed through the open plains and on 7th May Tunis fell. The battalion had followed the advancing troops and ended in their present position. Bill Pollock and I made our way over to the tented

Orderly Room to report in. On the notice board outside was pinned a copy of the signal sent by General Alexander to the Prime Minister, Winston Churchill. It was dated 10th May 1943 and stated: 'Sir, it is my duty to report that the Tunisian campaign is over. All enemy resistance has ended. We are masters of the North African Shore.'

CHAPTER 7

INTERLUDE IN NORTH AFRICA

I reported to Sergeant Kelly in the Orderly Room and he showed me the list of casualties, a copy of which he had already sent to RHQ in London. It was a long list, containing many friends. I looked down the Ds and there it was, Dempsey Michael, Killed in Action. Amongst the list of wounded in action were Kenneally J. and Pollock W. He crossed our names off this list. It was a start.

The battalion was only at company strength and it was to be nearly six months before we had four rifle companies again. There followed a very interesting time for all of us. We were given the temporary job of guarding Prisoners of War and there were thousands of them, both German and Italian. It was not unusual to see one solitary guardsman, armed only with a rifle and bayonet, escorting a column of 200 Italian POWs. They were easy to look after and were a great help in the running of the camp. They did all the fatigues and there were some great cooks in their number; we ate really well. They would even give you a shave whilst lying in bed if you asked – they would do anything to please. It boiled down to the fact that they were glad to be out of the war. Almost all of them were conscripts and all they wanted was to go back to their wives and bambinos in one piece. They disliked their officers and blamed them for the shambles they were in, and as for Mussolini, he and his cohorts should be hung up by their balls.

I only got to know one Italian officer, a major who was the Medical Officer. He was always immaculate and wore breeches and riding boots which were highly polished at all times. He was a middle-aged man who must have been soldiering for some time; from the number of medal ribbons he had it appeared he must have started his wars with Caesar. He would take medical parades twice a day as there were quite a number who had light wounds. He treated his men as if they were lower beings and they would jump to it when he bawled them out, which was often. Mind you, some of those Italian soldiers could show the worst of the guardsmen a thing or two about dodging the column.

I had been suffering from desert sores on the legs for some days. I had been to our own MO and he had treated me but the condition would not clear up. I visited the Italian Major. He had some greaseproof paper which he smeared with vaseline. He then sprinkled some white powder over the paper and wrapped it round the sores on my legs, bandaged them up and told me to come back in three days. I did, and when he peeled off the bandages my legs were as clear as a bell. A lot of the lads went to him with minor injuries. There was no doubt he knew his stuff.

With the Germans we were much more circumspect and they had to be watched. Many of them were still stuffed with the propaganda that had been fed them and the younger elements still believed that Rommel was going to come galloping over the hill and release them. It was easy to see the real Nazis, walking about with their noses in the air and keeping to their own groups. The older soldiers, especially those who had been on the Russian front, were quite eager to swap stories with us. None of them had much time for their Italian allies and they thought that we British felt the same about the Americans who had come late into the war and initially had made a few mistakes in their efforts in North Africa. They would give us little asides, like 'Spitfire come, we duck. Stuka come, you duck. Yankee bomber come, we both duck'. They respected their own officers and had lots of time for non-Nazi generals such as Rommel, Kesselring and Keitel.

It was most interesting to meet them but we were taken off these duties to prepare for the Victory Parade in Tunis. We were issued with new KD (khaki drill) and guardsmen's stiff caps; we spent hours cleaning and polishing, plus, as usual, we had extra drill to smarten us up. When the big day arrived, we seemed to stand for hours waiting for the inspection by the top brass: Churchill looking like a sack of potatoes in his drill suit, Anthony Eden looking as immaculate as ever befitting ex-Guards Office, Alexander, Omar Bradley, three French Generals, civic dignitaries, and hosts of British, American and French staff officers of all the service branches.

It was rumoured that as the Prime Minister stomped around our ranks he asked the CO if he had any Liverpool men in the regiment. 'I had some in the First World War. Keep your thumb on them. Keep your thumb on them.'

The march past was a bit of a shambles. There were American units, the French Foreign Legion and Moroccan Goums, whose style of marching was bizarre to say the least. The whole thing was topped off by French bands pounding away at about 140 beats – they were too enthusiastic even for the light infantry who were used to that sort of thing; and for us, used to 90 beats, it was all rather frustrating.

There followed the happy times while we recuperated from our efforts. Duties were light as we were very slowly being reinforced. I palled up with 'Grey Wolf' Broyan who, like myself, enjoyed watching the passing show, and there was plenty to see. We visited Tunis most days. Money was no object as we had not been paid for weeks and were now loaded with francs. Naturally we visited the kasbah and wandered through the dark allies and spent time in the bazaars and Arab shops. We were often pestered by young boys who asked for cigarettes and chocolate and we were offered the delights of their sisters and even themselves at the going rate. All this was new to me and I was glad to have the company of Broyan who had served in Egypt where this sort of thing was worse. Indeed, it was not uncommon for an unsuspecting soldier who succumbed to their offerings to end up with a knife between his shoulder blades, robbed and left in the dark alleyways.

We sampled all the bars along the Rue de Paris and drank tepid beer and muscatel with French Legionnaires and American soldiers from all states and we listened to the gripes of the Colonials. I had my first taste of the white-helmeted American Military Police, or Snowdrops as they were called. A group of GIs were getting stuck in to bottles of arrack, a white Arabian spirit which was raw and rough and burnt your guts as it went down. They got fighting drunk and started breaking the place up. The Snowdrops were sent for and they came wading in and thrashed these GIs unmercifully with their long night sticks, laying many of them out. They were particularly hard on a couple of black GIs, who to our knowledge had not been part of the ruck. We remonstrated with them over this and they started to reach for the .45 pistols at their hips. 'Out,' shouted Broyan, and out we went.

The Medical Officers had checked the local brothels and they were given the all-clear to reopen. There was a popular one called the 'Belvedere' and we would sit in the bar opposite and watch the goings-on. A queue would form before they opened, full of guys from all nations: black, white, yellow and even the odd Arab, just as if they were queueing for the cinema. One soldier at the head of the queue amused us greatly. He was a private in the Pioneer Corps; he was small with close-cropped ginger hair and wore thick-lensed glasses – only his mother could have loved him. He was first in and after a few minutes he was out again looking quite animated. He rejoined the queue and went in again – three times. After his last excursion he came over to the bar for a drink, his passion cooled. We joshed him about the number of times he'd been in. 'It was great,' he said in a thick Brummie accent, 'I'm going again tomorrow.'

All good things come to an end and so it was with our holiday in Tunis. We got a new Company Commander and Company Sergeant Major, and guardsmen were coming in from the reinforcement depot. Regular drills and parades started and discipline tightened up quickly as we began to reform.

They dished out the 'gongs' for the previous campaign. Captain Chesterton got the MC but we all felt he deserved more, Captain Fitzgerald, the Adjutant, received a well-earned MC. CQMS Mercer got a deserved Military Medal. The Commanders of 3 and 4 Companies were awarded the DSO and various other ranks received DCMs and MMs including, I was glad to see, Sergeant Musgrove who saved us that night with the 3" mortar. There was nothing for Liz Fanning or Sergeant Gundel, nor for Guardsman May who should have got an MM if only to stop him moaning. Liz was particularly upset: 'They're all bastards,' he said. 'If I'd been an officer I would have got a DSO; after all I did command No 1 Company on the hill.' I must admit to being slightly miffed myself. I thought I might have got a Military

Medal. Still, that's the way the cookie crumbles. I did get something, though – three stripes.

The new CSM, Gilmore (a nice guy, later killed at Anzio), called me into the office and said they were going to promote me to Lieutenant Sergeant. I said I did not want to be a Sergeant and was quite happy as I was. He well knew that as a Sergeant things changed. You came apart from the men; you did not eat with them or socialise and you used the Sergeants' Mess and mixed only with your own rank. From being one of 'us' you became one of 'them'. He told me not to be a bloody fool; the battalion was bound to change, all the survivors of the old battalion would be spread amongst the new companies and we would all be soldiering with new personnel just as he was. I took the stripes.

Things certainly did change. The battalion slowly filled up with new men and we carried on with the drill and tactical training. A memo appeared on the Sergeants' Mess notice-board which stated that a field selection board would be granting a commission of the rank of Second Lieutenant. Those wishing to apply were to attend CO orders. Liz Fanning, 'The Chief' Clem Gundel and myself applied.

The results were most interesting: Gundel was told he was too old – out. Kenneally was told he was a young man and his career lay with the regiment – out. It was different with Liz Fanning, though. He was always a thorn in the side of the officers and warrant officers but he knew Kings Regulations inside out and there was no doubting his ability as a soldier; he was in. Liz got a commission in the 'Buffs'. I met him a couple of years later at Euston station. He was a Captain then and it amused me greatly to see he was wearing a Guards Officer's cap with the regimental badge of the Buffs. He also spoke with a beautiful Oxbridge accent. There are none so pure as the purified.

Shortly after Liz Fanning left I was sent to Constantine for a month's course at the Allied School of Infantry. This was not unusual at that time in North Africa. All the Allies had learnt a lot from the African campaign and lots of our NCOs were sent here and there to pass on what we had learned and to learn from others. The Allied School of Infantry was run by the Americans and was attached to one of their infantry regiments stationed just outside Constantine, a really beautiful city originally built by the Romans. It was a fantastic place, steeped in history, and had not changed much over the centuries. We often marched through it and felt we were following the footsteps of the Roman Legions who had passed that way.

The idea of the course was to learn how to use each other's weapons and to learn each other's tactical ideas on the use of them. It was most interesting to compare my own battalion with an American one. Their discipline did not compare with ours – they did not have the fear of authority we had. I noticed junior officers and NCOs calling PFCs (Privates First Class) by their christian names. What was very noticeable was how they cliqued together according to their ancestry, Poles with Poles, Swedes with Swedes and Italians with Italians, etc. Guys from the Southern states were very insular too. My own regiment had a mixture of Northern and Southern Irish, English and a few Welsh and Scots. We also had cliques, but they were formed by the amount of service you had. Nationality did not come into it.

The American soldiers' kit was better than ours, the clothing better quality and well fitting and their boots excellent. We could not get on with American rations — everything tasted sweet, even the bread and bacon, and they drank mainly coffee. When tea was made for our benefit it was shocking. We lived and mixed with them and they bent over backwards to make us welcome and were generous to a fault. We British felt like poor relations in the face of this affluence. They taught us how to use their weapons and we taught them ours. We did tactical training and went over their assault courses with them, we marched together and had fun. They had piped music through the tents and loved Vera Lynn.

It was mid-August and I was in my last week there. We were busy cleaning our weapons after the day's training. The music stopped and the Allied Forces network news came over. I was only half-listening to the details of bombing raids here, there and everywhere. At the end of the news the announcer finished with the item that His Majesty King George VI had awarded the Victoria Cross to Lance Corporal

John Patrick Kenneally of the 1st Battalion Irish Guards. I listened to the citation in a daze. I just did not believe it. I had had to learn all the names of the Guards VCs at the Depot. Now my name would be added to them, and it was not really my name – I had adopted it.

When I had time to gather my thoughts I realised that keeping me from finding out about the VC in advance had required a lot of secrecy. When one knew the regiment as I did, where rumours were always rife and someone always knew the score before it happened, it must have taken some doing. I had not the faintest idea or inkling that my name had been put forward for this award. The CO knew, the Adjutant and the RSM room clerks knew, soldiers must have been interviewed by various officers, and yet it was done in such a way that the secret was kept.

I still had a few days to go with the Allied School of Infantry. VC or no VC I still had to clamber round their assault courses carrying a P16. I would not have had it any other way. The Yanks gave we British NCOs a great party the night before we left and they treated me as if I had won their own Congressional Medal of Honour. We left next morning to the tune of Vera Lynn's 'Yours' blaring out of the tannoy. We had all enjoyed the course. It was the first time I had lived and mixed with American soldiers and I was left with an affinity for them which never left me.

At the Battalion, still stationed outside Tunis, I had a

wonderful reception. Guys stopped what they were doing and crowded round to slap me on the back and shake my hand, shouting congratulations; it was a rare moment. We shared the honour and the glory of the Victoria Cross as we had shared the suffering, hardship and bloody murder of the *Bou*. There was no envy – infantrymen know better than that. It was not I who had won the medal: it was an Irish Guardsman. We were all Irish Guardsmen and we had all played a part.

I think the Sergeants' Mess party lasted three days, but naturally my recollections of this are a little hazy. Things soon got back to normal, though, and I returned to duty with my platoon. This was not to last as I was appointed Musketry Sergeant and transferred to HQ Company. This was a plum job in an infantry battalion and usually given only to a Sergeant with much longer service than I. I jumped at it – no more boring guard duties, no more PT, and very few drill parades.

I needed the extra spare time. Large packages of mail kept arriving for me and I realised that I was a celebrity, at least for the time being. I received letters of congratulation from people all over the world including Canada, South Africa, Australia, New Zealand and America. One sack arrived containing well over 2,000 items from the UK and Southern Ireland. Reading these letters made me realise how little I knew of the world, how little of the grief and suffering of others, how little I knew of the ideals at stake in the war we were waging. Wrapped up in the cocoon of my regiment I knew nothing and felt that I needed another ten or fifteen years on my shoulders before I could answer some of them. There were letters from wives, mothers and sweethearts of men killed in action, letters from widows of the First World War, and a very moving letter from Lady Lyell, the widow of the Scots Guards Officer who won a VC shortly before myself. Reading these I felt guilty to be alive. There were letters from relatives of soldiers I was serving with, asking me to look out for them. On the lighter side I heard from girlfriends I had met along the way, and there was a formal note from my father congratulating me; how ironic that he who was decorated in the First World War could not publicly acknowledge me now.

Amongst the congratulations from Ireland were many from ex-Irish Guards, men of the Great War, and a kind letter from the family with whom I had spent a leave in Dublin. The Irish love a hero and jokingly they wrote that they were going to put a notice in the window saying 'Kenneally stayed here'. I was amused by letters from unknown relatives who said I was their third or fourth cousin and must be a son of Uncle Michael who they had not known of for years. Written on a page torn out of an exercise book was a roughly written note from Co. Galway. It read: 'Dear Golden Balls, You did us proud.' It was signed Halloran. From a chancer like him, who did not believe in anything, and who had made it possible for me to join the regiment, it was a real accolade.

All good things come to an end and the sweet life around Tunis ended abruptly with orders for the battalion to rejoin the 1st Division for training on the south coast of Cap Bon. Our destination was Hammamet, a distance of some fifty miles, and we were to march it in two days. That march was the worst I was ever to experience in all my soldiering. It was the height of the African summer and blazing hot. We sweated profusely and the water carriers were much in demand. I was sorry for the guys I was with, who were all reinforcements and had only arrived two days before. They were completely unacclimatised and were suffering from the heat, so they drank too much water which made things worse. There is a knack to desert soldiering and it takes an infantryman at least three months to learn the art. These guardsmen had to do it the hard way and it says much for their spirit and discipline that at the end of the march they were still there and in reasonable order.

An added hazard was the choking dust kicked up by frequent Arab convoys of lorries which sped past us, piled high with their goods and chattels. There was a lot of Arab movement from Tunis at this time and I can only suppose they had been consorting with the German forces and were escaping from retribution by their French colonial masters. They certainly were not pro-British because they shouted remarks and made insulting gestures as they drove past. Not unnaturally, the lads reciprocated in no uncertain manner.

A typical incident happened when we were 'taking five' just in front of a bridge. An Arab convoy came up fast and the leading lorry was piled high with mattresses on top of which stood a young Arab who was busy giving us the usual derisory two-fingered salute and shouting, 'Up yours, Tommy.' He forgot one thing – the bridge. Ignoring our shouts to duck, which he probably did not understand, he hit the bridge head high and must have been killed instantly. His compatriots in the following trucks just ran over him as if he were a rabbit on the road and left us to pick up the pieces as they disappeared in a cloud of dust. Life is cheap in Africa.

Hammamet was fantastic. We bivouaced just sixty yards from the sea with olive groves and fig trees for shade. Reveille was at 4.45am and we would sprint across the golden beaches for a quick dip in the sea before first parade. The afternoon heat was very oppressive and we could do little but float in the warm sea or take afternoon siestas. In the cold of the evening we would drink red wine and hold impromptu concerts. It was great to be a soldier and I never felt fitter – if we had only had female company life would have been idyllic.

It was decided that I would be presented with the ribbon of the Victoria Cross by General Alexander on 27th August. For a description of this ceremony, I am pleased to rely on the official history of the Irish Guards:

THIRD SUPPLEMENT
TO
The London Gazette
Of FRIDAY, the 13th of AUGUST, 1943
Published by Authority

Registered as a newspaper

TUESDAY, 17 AUGUST, 1943

War Office, 17th August, 1943.

The KING has been graciously pleased to approve the award of the VICTORIA CROSS to:—

No. 2722925 Lance-Corporal John Patrick Kenneally, Irish Guards (Tipton, Staffs.).

The Bou feature dominates all ground East and West between Medjez El Bab and Tebourba. It was essential to the final assault on Tunis that this feature should be captured and held.

A Guards Brigade assaulted and captured a portion of the Bou on the 27th April, 1943. The Irish Guards held on to points 212 and 214 on the Western end of the feature, which points the Germans frequently counter-attacked. While a further attack to capture the complete feature was being prepared, it was essential for the Irish Guards to hold on. They did so.

On the 28th April, 1943, the positions held by one Company of the Irish Guards on the ridge between points 212 and 214 were about to be subjected to an attack by the enemy. Approximately one Company of the enemy were seen forming up preparatory to attack and Lance-Corporal Kenneally decided that this was the right moment to attack them himself. Single-handed he charged down the bare forward slope straight at the main enemy body firing his Bren gun from the hip as he did so. This outstanding act of gallantry and the dash with which it was executed completely unbalanced the enemy Company which broke up in disorder. Lance-Corporal Kenneally then returned to the crest further to harass their retreat.

Lance-Corporal Kenneally repeated this remarkable exploit on the morning of the 30th April, 1943, when, accompanied by a Sergeant of the Reconnaissance Corps, he again charged the enemy forming up for an assault. This time he so harassed the enemy,

inflicting many casualties, that this projected attack was frustrated: the enemy's strength was again about one Company. It was only when he was noticed hopping from one fire position to another further to the left, in order to support another Company, carrying his gun in one hand and supporting himself on a Guardsman with the other, that it was discovered he had been wounded. He refused to give up his Bren gun, claiming that he was the only one who understood that gun, and continued to fight all through that day with great courage, devotion to duty and disregard for his own safety.

The magnificent gallantry of this N.C.O. on these two occasions, under heavy fire, his unfailing vigilance, and remarkable accuracy were responsible for saving many valuable lives during the days and nights in the forward positions. His actions also played a considerable part in holding these positions and this influenced the whole course of the battle. His rapid appreciation of the situation, his initiative and his extraordinary gallantry in attacking single-handed a massed body of the enemy and breaking up an attack on two occasions, was an achievement that can seldom have been equalled. His courage in fighting all day when wounded was an inspiration to all ranks.

'A tremendous day,' wrote Colonel Scott. 'General Alexander arrived accompanied by the Corps Commander, the Divisional Commander, Lieutenant-General Bradley of the US Army and Major General Leinnitzer, the American Deputy Chief of Staff. The battalion was formed up on three sides of a square in a rather dusty field and under a very hot sun. The place was stiff with reporters and photographers. We had no idea what sort of a parade General Alexander wanted but he said on arrival that he wanted to go round the whole battalion. He did this, and then Kenneally was marched up to him through the battalion by RSM McLoughlin. After he had pinned the ribbon on Sergeant Kenneally, he made a speech to the battalion, congratulating them personally on having played a vital part in his victory, and probably total victory. Then he ordered the battalion to march past while he stood at the saluting base with Sergeant Kenneally on his right.'

My feelings for the regiment on this great occasion were very mixed. I felt very composed and almost detached from it all. I am no modest fool. I had shown courage and here I was getting a medal for it, not just a medal but the highest honour for valour my country can bestow. The only pride I felt was that intimate personal pride of every soldier in the fact that he had been tried and tested in battle and not found wanting. I stood amongst the beribboned Generals and studied the sweating faces of my comrades as they marched by. I saw the faces of the dead in the ranks: Mickey

Dempsey, the gallant Sergeant Salt, Lieutenant Eugster, Detchfield and McCluskey, all of whom had been recruits with me at the Guards Depot – so many comrades who had all shown courage and paid the ultimate price. More than pride, I felt humility. As the last company marched by my mood changed. I thought you need 25 per cent courage and 75 per cent luck. Being half a Jew, I must be one of the chosen people.

Needless to say, we had a ball in the Sergeants' Mess that night, which took me two days to get over. That parade sparked off quite a busy time for me. I received orders to report to the British Ambassador's residence at La Marsa on the outskirts of Tunis. That magnificent house had been taken over as General Alexander's headquarters. I was to have an official portrait painted by Captain H. M. Carr, the war artist. I sat on ammunition boxes dressed in full khaki drill and battle order. The light was perfect and I had sittings of two to three hours each day. It took him twelve days to complete. I was not too thrilled with the result; but it was hung in the Imperial War Museum for many years until they got bored with it.

Whilst at La Marsa I had an insight into how large armies were organised and administered. The place was littered with high-ranking staff officers and I got sick and tired of saluting. The house was occupied by the heavy brass, with other ranks in tented accommodation at the rear. I shared a tent with a master cook of the Army Catering Corps and he naturally ensured we had the same food as the generals. The fare was superb and the wines more so. The gardens were beautiful and very well tended by the numerous Arab gardeners. The best times were the evenings with the heavy scent of jasmine in the air and a stomach full of good food and wine. All was well with the world and it wasn't half great to be a soldier.

I met quite a few of the war correspondents, both British and American, and I was not particularly impressed with the British ones; all they seemed to care about was the heat and where the next gin and tonic was coming from. I became friendly with an American correspondent from Philadelphia, who apart from sending reports home also wrote articles for *Stars and Stripes*, the American Forces Magazine. As a result of our conversations he must have written an article about the Allied School of Infantry which I had attended. Some months later I received a letter from the American commandant of the school, thanking me for the good remarks I had made about it. On the whole, American reporters took much more interest in what the ordinary soldier had to say than their British counterparts.

I was not sorry to leave La Marsa when the time came – fine living is no substitute for the camaraderie of your own regiment.

Soon after my return to the battalion, rumours began to circulate that we would soon be on the move again and they were right; we were going to Italy to take our part in that campaign. We were not displeased – the weather was changing and everyone was a little bored with North Africa. So what if we were going into action again – we were soldiers and that was what we were paid for. The battalion moved out on 27th November for 'Texas Staging Area' just outside Bizerta, where they went under canvas and waited for transport by sea to Italy. I clicked for the job of rear party. I had twelve guardsmen and a corporal and was to tidy up the site, remove all the rubbish the battalion had left behind and leave it in good order. A truck would come and pick us up in a couple of days to join the battalion for embarkation.

The last truck had hardly disappeared in a cloud of dust when the local Arab *muktah* came to see me. My Arabic was poor, his English more so. He did speak a little French and, with my schoolboy French, we were able to communicate during our near three-month stay at Hammamet. Our cooks had begged, borrowed or stolen a large Nissen hut which they had used as a food store and cookhouse. My Arab friend wanted it as a residence for his three wives and family – it would be a great improvement on his present mud hut.

'If I give you this Nissen hut,' I said, 'what will you do for me?' He thought long and hard and came up with the proposal that his wives and family would clean up the site for us and burn all the rubbish. In addition, he would supply us with any eggs, tomatoes or bread we needed and his fifteen-year-old unmarried daughter would do any washing

I might require and make herself useful round the camp. I thought hard about his offer, especially the last part. Luckily, my command consisted of young reinforcements: I would not have given tuppence for the girl's chances of remaining a virgin if they had been my ex-comrades of No 1 Company. 'OK,' I said, 'it's yours.' He wanted some title to the hut. On a piece of notepaper I wrote: 'This Nissen hut is the sole property of Ali Bin Said, for services rendered.' I put the company stamp on it and signed it, Tom Micks, Officer Commanding. He was very impressed with this and I was to be his friend for life. He also invited us to his eldest daughter's wedding celebration, to be held the following evening. He would probably have got away with that Nissen hut; to the best of my knowledge the site would never be occupied again.

He was as good as his word and the site was made immaculate. The little girl, Nadia, did my washing and pressed my KD. She was shy and would not look at anyone directly, but after a lot of coaxing and leg-pulling she became more confident. Ten of us went to the Arab wedding. I left the corporal and two men to guard our bivouacs and arms. Although I liked my Arab friend, I did not trust his compatriots: they had the ability to appear and disappear like shadows in the night. Nothing was too hot or too heavy to be carried away.

The wedding party was fun but nothing elaborate. Our hosts were poor peasants, but what they had, they shared with us. Two separate large fires had been lit in the centre of the village compound. The men sat round one, the women the other. Music was supplied by reed pipes and a leather drum and the feast consisted of goat meat stew served in communal brass dishes, flat Arab bread, sticky sweet cakes, fresh figs and dates. The women moved amongst us serving red wine, arrack which was almost 100 per cent proof, and sweet, mint-tasting coffee. As the wine flowed the music got faster and the bolder amongst the women would dance round the fires accompanied by those shrill Arabic wails that the women seemed to specialise in; young boys would dance as well but never the men. I think it was a double celebration; they rejoiced not only in the wedding but also in the restoration — with the end of war, and the departure of the British troops — of the normal pattern of their lives.

A battered old Isotta Fraschini truck rolled up to take us back to the battalion. It was 3rd December. The whole village turned out to see us off; much to Nadia's pride and gratification we heaped on her our spare chocolate and toilet soap (this was highly prized). She shed genuine tears as she waved us goodbye.

As the truck trundled down the track my last view of them was of the muktah moving his family into his new manor house. I visited the same village some forty years on; things were much the same except there was a television aerial sticking out of each mud hut.

The truck driver was an old regular corporal whom I

knew well and he filled me in on the news of the battalion. It seemed that the main body was encamped outside Bizerta and due to leave the next day. Our destination was to be Taranto in the heel of Italy. We drove through Tunis to take a last look. Gone were the teeming troops of all nations; the French Colonial police had taken over, and the city was much cleaner and back to normal. We were not unhappy to see the back of it. The cost in comrades had been very high.

CHAPTER 8

AN ITALIAN OCCUPATION

We crossed the Mediterranean sea peacefully; after passing quite close to Sicily, we crossed the Gulf of Taranto to land on Tuesday 7th December 1943. The battalion disembarked in good spirits; it was great to be back in Europe. We formed up on the quay at Taranto; I was now with Headquarters Company. The Company Sergeant Majors roared for quiet, the Drill Sergeants added their dulcet tones, the Pipers opened up with a few quivering wails (which frightened the watching Italian children and onlookers). RSM McLoughlin called the battalion to attention, we sloped arms and with Colonel Scott leading we moved off through the streets of Taranto and into Italy, to the Regimental march 'St Patrick's Day'.

Road blocks and rusty barbed wire had been left everywhere by the retreating German army. There was an air of poverty and dereliction about the town. The local population – with their lowered eyes and sullen manner – did not look overjoyed to see us. As we hit the countryside we marched at ease and took stock of our surroundings; olive trees lined the roads and we passed a good mile of tomato fields from which came the most appalling stench. Drably dressed women and children were working between the rows. One of the lads who reckoned he knew about such things claimed they fertilised the fields with their own excreta. It was enough to put me off Italian tomatoes for life. The staging camp was a further two miles up the road and we were grateful to drop our heavy packs, pitch tents and take a rest.

That evening a couple of recreational trucks were laid on for a visit to Taranto; Sgt. Gundel, Sgt. George Murphy (Spud) and myself scrambled aboard. Spud Murphy had joined us in Africa as a reinforcement; he was a 'Brummie' yet came from an Irish Guards family – his father had been a CSM at the Guards' Depot and Spud was a regular who had joined the regiment at seventeen. He was small for a guardsman but as tough as teak; we became close friends but sadly it was not a friendship that was to last. Taranto had nothing to offer, mainly because they had nothing. Money was of no use as everything worked on a barter system; a bar of chocolate would enable you to drink as much of the coarse red vino as you could drink, a packet of cigarettes supplied a meal of poor quality for three, five cigarettes would buy you a woman, and for a bar of soap you could have as many trashy religious trinkets as you wanted. There was an air of defeat and depression, far from the natural gaiety and love of life that I was to find amongst the Italian people later; it was not a happy place in that cold winter of 1943.

Next day we boarded an Italian train bound for Canosa, near Bari on the Adriatic coast; this move reinforced the rumour that we were to join the Eighth Army, who were ensconced in the mountains beyond Foggia. The train was very slow and we travelled all night and half a day before reaching Canosa. We were marched about six miles to a very large granary surrounding a courtyard. The men were billeted in the granaries with the officers using the farmhouse. Our billets were full of charred ammunition boxes and burnt-out ration tins left by the Germans. We cleaned and whitewashed the place in two days. We found some stoves and warmed it up. It was infinitely better than pitching tents in the hard frozen grounds, as we were to spend Christmas and the New Year of 1944 there.

On Christmas Eve, Spud Murphy and I, being bored out of our minds, decided to hitch a lift to Bari to find some action. We were not the only ones: quite a few guardsmen and some junior officers were on the same tack. Bari was a large Adriatic seaside resort and was an American forces town; all the bars were packed with GIs and Marines and we were very much in the minority. Four of my pals from No 1 Company, accompanied by two American marines who they had palled up with, joined me and Spud at the bar; there was 'Hopper' Adamson (a fearless Geordie who I had been in many a scrape with), Montgomery, Grey Wolf, Brogan and Bill Pollock, who had shared the same machine-gun burst with me. Hopper said, 'These two guys know a smashing place about half a mile away. Come on, Johnno, we'll have some fun.'

Against our better judgment we joined them. As we approached the stucco building in the back streets our misgivings increased; plastered all over were the signs, 'Out of Bounds to all Military Personnel', 'Strictly Forbidden'; there were even German 'Verboten' signs which had not been taken down. I smelt trouble. Monty said, 'It doesn't say anything about the British.' We entered.

It was a brothel, but they had American beer and rye whisky supplied, no doubt, by grateful GI quartermasters, and there was a pianist who thumped out Yankee tunes. The Madame was very interested in us; I think we were the first British troops who had been in there. The girls admired our height and size, but they were a very lousy lot, and it was obvious that if you wanted a dose of clap this was the place to come. The beer and wine flowed, we sang 'O Sole Mio' with the piano player and were getting pleasantly drunk when there was a squeal of brakes outside, a hammering on the door and then it was kicked in. A posse of a dozen baton-wielding 'Snowdrops' poured in. With shouts of 'Stay where you are' two guarded the door, some thumped upstairs and the rest rushed through to the back entrance to catch the GIs baling out. The Madame was cursing the American Military Police Sergeant, the girls were screaming for their money and the GIs were trying to escape in all directions. There was no sign of our two erstwhile Marine pals.

With a concerted rush the six of us knocked the two

Snowdrops who were guarding the front door out of the way and we all baled out. Monty, who had the instincts of a fox, whipped open the door of the armoured car that was parked outside – in their rush the MPs had left the key in it. We piled in and with a scrunch of gears Monty pulled away. The bastards opened up on us – .45 slugs slammed into the rear doors and they even fired at us from the upstairs windows of the brothel. Monty rounded the corner and we were away with no harm done; there were bullet holes in the roof but no one was hit so we proceeded on our merry way back to Canosa. We parked the wagon about half a mile from the granaries and walked back just in time to join midnight mass in the chapel attached to the farm house. It had been a good night out.

Christmas Day opened with no repercussions and the battalion enjoyed itself. The Master Cook, Sgt. Kennedy, had produced a magnificent meal: we had roast pork and turkey and it was as good a Christmas Day as ever we had in England. Boxing Day was a different matter, though. I spotted an American Military Police vehicle parked outside battalion HQ. By dint of questioning I learned that an American Provost-marshal was closeted with the Adjutant and RSM McLaughlin – they had obviously found their vehicle. Through Sgt. Kelly from the Orderly Room, who was a friend, I learnt what had happened; it seemed some soldiers identified as guardsmen had taken a vehicle from Bari on Christmas Eve. RSM McLaughlin, who would defend his battalion to the death, said all his men were God-fearing Catholics who had attended Mass on the Christmas Eve — it must have been those unbelievers in the Scots or Grenadier Guards who were the culprits. After a couple of glasses of Christmas cheer the Provost-marshal left quite happily, and that was the end of the affair.

Orders were received that the 1st Division were to relieve the 8th Indian Division on the 8th Army Front and an advance party was to be sent up there. On New Year's Eve we had a party in the Sergeants' Mess; we had not got much but someone had hired a three-piece Italian band who only knew Italian music. But we made do and drank red vino.

New Year's Day opened with the issue of the African Star ribbon and everyone got busy with the sewing needles. In the afternoon who should roll up but thirty musicians of the Regimental Band who had been touring Italy entertaining various commands. We looked forward to an evening's entertainment, but it was not to be. About 6.30 that evening there was frenzied activity and much shouting of commands — the battalion was to move out that night. At 8.30 there was to be full Roll Call; every man-jack had to parade in full pack order. I stood at the rear of HQ Company and watched. It was like a scene from a Twentieth Century Fox film. We stood in the freezing cold and it was snowing slightly. The job of calling the battalion roll was given to CSM Stewart, who had the finest word of command and diction in the regiment; as each man's name was called, he had to spring to attention and shout 'Sir'.

The names had a legendary quality: Alexander, Fitzgerald, Fitzpatrick, Fitzsimons, Mahoney, Murphy, A. B. & C. Kelly, D. F. G. Lavery, O'Shaughnessy, O'Neill, McNulty, McGarry, Rafferty, Montgomery, Brogan, Pollock, G. & W. Adamson, Kenny, Kennedy – even my own adopted name Kenneally had a ring to it. With a crash of steel-tipped boots on the cobblestones the battalion was called to attention and the Commanding Officer addressed us. All previous orders were countermanded; the battalion was to join the 5th American army under General Mark Clark for an amphibious landing – where we would be informed later. He wished us good fortune; we sloped arms and moved out to our transport. It was an occasion. The CO must have felt like Caesar; we certainly felt like Roman legionnaires about to set out on another campaign.

On 2nd January the battalion drove across Italy to Gragnan, a small town on the south side of the Bay of Naples. We started out at 03.30 hours and were the last in the convoy. Just before we reached Foggia it became light, the dawn of a clear sunny day. By about seven o'clock we could clearly see everything to the mountains on the promontory of Manfredouca. It was a memorable journey through the green valleys and snow-topped mountains by Ariano and Avellino.

From Avellino the road down into the valley was precipitous giving an aerial view of miles of countryside. The snow was thawing on the streets of the villages; our lorries skated into ditches and occasionally skidded into the walls of the houses, much to the wails and laments of the Italian owners and much to our amusement. Just as it was beginning to get dark we came up over the last hills and a strong pungent smell hit us in the face; it was Naples. We caught our first glimpse of Vesuvius with thin wispy smoke coming from the summit, passed through San Severino, Pompeii, and Castellammare and dismounted at Gragnano.

We were billeted in a huge disused spaghetti factory in the main street of the town and the large drying rooms turned themselves into ready-made large barracks. The battalion was to stay there over two weeks. The rifle companies practised their drill, went on route marches and we did one 'Combined Operations' exercise which was a bit of a shambles. It was obvious to all and sundry that a large invasion force was being gathered in Castellammare harbour but no one yet knew where it was going.

Rumours were rife as usual; Corsica, Yugoslavia, the South of France, North of Rome, South of Rome – all were mentioned one time or another. We were not over-worried. Wherever we were about to land, it would be no picnic for us; despite the bravado, in each man's mind was the knowledge that he might not come back. But if he was going to die he was going to have a good time before the call came.

Most of the lads went in to Naples, which was supposed to be swinging; some went to Sorrento.

Spud Murphy and I decided to try Castellammare which was just three or four miles away. As we walked into the outskirts of the port we fell in behind two girls who were strolling along; we both studied them from behind. One was tall for an Italian girl and had almost fair hair, the other was small and very dark. Even though they were wearing heavy coats as it was very cold, we could see they had good figures. 'Let's chat them up,' said Spud. 'You go for the tall one, I'll go for shorty – she's more my size.' We stepped up beside them and saw that they were both good-looking girls – Spud and I perked up, started the usual banter; the language of courtship is universal and with the bits of halting Italian we had picked up we were able to communicate. It was very pleasant to have pretty female company after a year of celibacy.

By the time we reached the town centre we knew each other's names. I was John, later to become Johnny, the tall girl was Maria, Spud was George, later to become Georgio, and the dark girl was Rosa. I asked if they could direct us to a decent cafe where we could get something to eat and drink. They took us off the main street which was littered with bars; 'No good, bad place,' they said, and took us through the back streets to a cafe that was near the quay. We asked them to come in with us but they both refused; 'No, no,' they said, 'we're married,' and pointed to their wedding rings, which neither of us had noticed.

We cajoled them but they were adamant. As a last resort we tried the old trick; our pockets were stuffed with chocolate and cigarettes for bartering and Maria, who I found later had quite a mercenary streak, was impressed when I gave her a bar. After a lot of jabber jabber between them they came in with us. They were indeed married but both their husbands had been conscripted into Mussolini's African legions and they had heard nothing of them for over a year. After seeing the thousands of Italian soldiers in the bay in North Africa we consoled them with the fact that they were most probably prisoners of war and would hear from them eventually; to be honest they did not seem over worried.

It turned out to be a great night – the bar and cafe was mainly used by the fishermen who were nearly all middle aged or old men; most of the young males had gone off to war and little was known of their fates. Mussolini and Fascism were dirty words and they hated the Germans who had ridden rough shod over them and looted and requisitioned what little they had.

We left the cafe around midnight. The owner gave me a bottle of Italian cognac (in exchange for cigarettes) and promised to be my friend for life. All four of us were three sheets to the wind and we staggered to Maria's house for coffee. I say house – it consisted of two rooms, a living room and bedroom; there was no heating, only a charocoal brazier in the living room which also served for cooking. There were two oil lamps for lighting; the water tap and privy were both outside. I came to realise later how poor Southern Italy really was. Maria made the ersatz coffee and we followed with a cognac.

It had been obvious for half an hour that Spud and Rosa had other things on their minds and they left together; Rosa only lived two doors away. Maria looked at me and said in her fractured English: 'We go sleep now yes.' What a question. We both stripped off in the lamplight and dived under the heaped blankets – it was very cold. She wrapped her arms around me immediately: she was hungry for a man. I don't know how long it had been for her but it had been too long for me. I wanted her badly. She carried a slight smell of garlic which was slightly off-putting but who was I to be so pernickety. We made love long and hard and then slept soundly in each other's arms.

I was woken by Spud banging on the front door: 'Come on, Roll Call is at 8am.' I dressed quickly. Maria said she would meet me at 6pm that evening outside the factory. We sprinted up the road and with the help of a lift on a ration truck we made the parade quite easily. 'How was it, Spud?' I asked. 'Smashing,' he replied. 'I'm seeing her again tonight.' He was already half in love with Rosa.

During the afternoon I had a bath in the makeshift showers the Pioneers had set up. I noticed some little red marks on my chest: they were flea bites. Jesus Christ, I was lousy. I must have got them in Maria's bed. But, fleas or no fleas, I wanted more of that woman.

I washed my underwear and put on a fresh set. I got a large tin of disinfestation powder from the Medic Sergeant and dusted all the seams of my battledress and my great-coat; the tin I would give to Maria and she could sort that bed out. At 6pm the two girls were waiting for us outside the Guardroom. I told them about the flea episode and they both giggled like schoolgirls: it would appear that fleas were a fact of life with them and nothing to get upset about. Maria taught me a lot; I learnt about Mussolini and his Blackshirts, how he fancied himself as the greatest Roman Emperor of all time, how he encouraged large families, to supply cannon fodder for his grandiose schemes. Women who had ten children or more were given a medal; conscription had been in since 1936 and his victories in Abyssinia and Eritrea had only served to reinforce his ambitions. The older men talked sadly of the happier days under the old Italian aristocracy; they had swopped one set of masters for a worse lot. Anyone who opposed the regime disappeared mysteriously in the night.

Disillusion swiftly set in when *Il Duce* jumped on Hitler's bandwagon and declared war on the Allies. Many Italians had migrated to America and Britain and thousands worked in France; Maria's own eldest brother was in London and had a family, and a branch of Rosa's family had been in New York since before the First World War.

The German forces had treated them as second-class citizens and on their retreat had bled them dry. They lived from day to day; civil government had broken down; there was no communication with relatives in the forces, and the rationing system had collapsed. The black market ruled. I was to see the same pattern, only much worse, in Germany later.

Spud and I supplied the girls with what we could beg, borrow and forage and indeed when the inevitable time came for us to leave we left them (in black market terms) wealthy young women. In return they gave us two young infantry soldiers love, companionship and lots of fun; for Spud it was the last he was to have.

Ominously, the battalion received a visit from the Corps Commander – a Major General Lucas of the US Army. He seemed quite old and a fatherly figure; he said how proud he was to have such a regiment under his command, what great blokes we were and how it was going to be easy. When a General tells a soldier that, he smells trouble.

Castellammare bay was crammed with ships and the battalion was to embark on the 20th January. After a night of love and fun we said our goodbyes. Maria said she would light a candle for me every day and call on all the saints to protect me; her last words were: 'Come back, Johnny, and take me away from this place.' Spud and Rosa were very much in love and there were tears all round as we kissed goodbye.

The battalion paraded in full fighting order in the broad street of Gragnano. The regimental band which had followed us to the town gave a short concert in the town square whilst we were forming up. At 1400 hours, headed by the regimental band, we marched out of Gragnano and down the hill to Castellammare to the tune of 'St Patrick's Day'. I was amazed to see the Italians lining the street cheering and clapping us on our way. I realised that many of the guardsmen had Italian girlfriends amongst the cheering crowd; many of these walked in step with their soldiers and gave them flowers and trinkets. As we approached the centre of Castellammare the band struck up 'The Minstrel Boy' and with the ringing sound of the guardsmen's steady pace on the cobblestones a sense of occasion overtook all of us. As we passed the saluting plinth in the centre of the square Colonel Scott returned our 'eyes left' salute. Maria ran out of the crowd and pressed a golden St Christopher medallion into my hand. To the tune of 'Wearing of the Green', we marched into the port and up the ramps of the boats. Most certainly if a man was going to war this was the way to do it – with pomp and circumstance. I thought it would be a long time before the local populace forgot that they had played host to the 1st Battalion Irish Guards.

Support Company and the transport were already loaded in their tank landing craft. The rifle companies filed up the ramps on to their infantry landing craft – long, narrow, shallow-draught ships like miniature corvettes. These landing craft were troop-carrying egg shells; apart from the engines there was nothing inside them but three large cabins fitted with old wooden tram seats into which it is possible to cram 120 men loaded with equipment. Carrying rifles, Bren guns, Stens and Tommy guns, Piats and bombs, mortars and bombs, wireless sets, camp kettles, water cans and rations, the guardsmen stumbled down the narrow iron ladders into the cabins. The officers were further burdened by long rolls of maps which they were not to distribute till the convoy had set sail. It was terribly crowded below decks. Somehow or other they sorted themselves out and found a place for their equipment and their bodies. 'Can we smoke?' was always the first question. There was nothing to do but wait and smoke, smoke and wait, till the Navy put them onshore again. The officers urged the men to get some sleep as it might be the last chance for a long time, but only physical exhaustion could bring sleep in such quarters.

The convoy assembled in Naples Bay. There were ships as far as the eye could see. LCIs, LCTs, small craft, landing ships, MTBs, mine sweepers, destroyers, an aircraft carrier and a couple of cruisers.

About 7 o'clock the convoy sailed. It headed out to sea through the channel between Cape Corrento and the Island of Capri and then steamed south, a ruse to deceive any German reconnaissance planes. A destroyer with General Alexander on the bridge cut through the lone line of ships flying the signal 'Good Luck to you all'. At dusk the convoy turned on its tracks and steamed north up the coast. It was a dark, still winter night. There was no moon but the stars gave enough light to see the dark outlines of the ships and the faint phosphorescent glow of their wakes. It was eerily quiet. Standing on deck it was possible to hear a low murmur from the cabins. We watched the dark Italian coast slip by; we passed the mouth of the River Gariyliana and could hear distant thuds and see pin-point flashes of gunfire.

Meanwhile, below decks, the company commanders on each of the landing craft were unrolling the maps and preparing their briefings. We crowded into the largest cabin. The officer shone a light on the large scale map of Italy and began. 'We are landing at a place called Anzio tomorrow morning. Anzio, here it is, thirty miles south of Rome. This is what is going to happen . . .'

CHAPTER 9

ASSAULT ON ANZIO

We reached Anzio just after midnight on Saturday 22nd January. The submarines *Ultor* and *Uproar* were waiting as markers, on either side of the port. Naval scout parties were sent ashore to signpost the beaches. At 2am the rocket ships broke the silence and hammered each side and the rear of the beaches. There was no reply from the shore and the first 'wave' of assault troops went in (we had drawn a long straw and were to be in the third wave). The first wave were the North Staffs and Gordon Highlanders. I wondered if that white-haired major with the shepherd's crook was wading ashore with his 'wee' Gordons. Still no response from the enemy. An hour later the second wave, consisting of 1st Battalion the Loyals and 1st Battalion Scots Guards went in. Still nothing; we heard no firing whatsoever. Around 3am the silence was broken by the chatter of the wireless and we heard that surprise had been complete and everything was going well.

The moon rose and from the decks out at sea we could observe the coastline and the officers pointed out landmarks. We had to sit and wait it out until the assault brigades had secured the initial bridgehead. The Loyals advanced north west along the coast road to Cafforella seven miles from Anzio. On the right flank the Scots Guards advanced down the road towards Anzio. In the centre the North Staffs and the Gordons advanced north towards the Campo de Carne and plunged into the tangled wilderness of the woods called Selva di Nettuno. The Commandos and American Rangers landed at Anzio itself and easily captured the dock area.

I did not even get my feet wet – the whole battalion landed on Anzio dry shod. 'Ducks' (large amphibious jeeps) ferried us to floating pontoons and we walked up the sandy track to the coast road and then on between the trees towards Anzio. The Adjutant, Captain Fitzgerald, checked each company individually as they passed by; no one had fallen overboard. We passed Italian farm labourers on their way to work. 'Dove Tedeschi,' we asked. 'Niente Tedeschi,' they replied and jerked their thumbs vaguely north west – 'Roma'. So the Germans were in Rome just thirty miles up the road. The battalion halted in the roadside woods with the Grenadiers between them and the main Anzio-Albano road. This was a wide, well-made road, typically Roman, open and as straight as an arrow, and an observer on the hills could see the entire length of it. It was the only main road leading north and the only short cut to Rome. The beachhead centred on this road; all the fighting in the following weeks consisted of fierce attempts by the Allies to extend their hold on it and to foil German attempts to cut it.

We stretched out in the woods to await developments; but there were none. When the sun went down it turned bitterly cold. The battalion transport had not yet been unloaded so we had no shelter. A chilling mist rose from the dark wood, water dripped from the trees and soaked us, then water seeped up from the ground and by midnight was frozen. After a year in Africa we were not used to it. It was too cold to sleep and this was to be a long miserable night. How I longed for Maria's loving arms and warm bed. Right then, I'd have gladly coped with the fleas.

About 4am Drill Sergeant Kenny, myself and two other NCOs were ordered to go down to the harbour and see what had happened to our transport. I was glad of something to do and the march down to the harbour warmed us up. We found our transport alright, at the back of the queue; being the third wave ashore, our transport was at the rear. By dint of much cursing and cajoling, Captain Egan, the MT Officer, winkled out the small 15cwt Bedford platoon trucks and sent them on ahead. When we arrived with the 3 tonners the tinned bacon was sizzling and the tea brewing, each man had his greatcoat and blanket and we felt a lot better. But then it started to rain.

What were we messing about at? Rome was only thirty miles up the road; we could have been drinking vino with the Pope by now. The delay and inaction caused unconcealed disquiet amongst the battalion. Officers and men discussed it endlessly. It was the only thing to do in the sodden freezing woods. We all had a sickening feeling of anti-climax; each and every one of us had been keyed up for a bold advance on Rome. It might have been rough and bloody but we would have got there. We had the element of surprise. There were no Germans. What in the name of God was stopping the Division advancing? We could not fathom it, and the officers were dismayed at the turn of events. There were the usual answers: the necessity of securing a firm base before advancing, the need for landing and accumulating supplies, the inadvisability of doing anything rash. We were not convinced; our opinion was that the American division on our right flank wanted to get there first and were not ready yet; after all it was an American operation and commanded by them. This opinion was borne out by subsequent events. Who can ever forget the newsreel pictures of General Mark Clark leading his victorious Fifth Army into Rome?

The twenty-third of January was a completely wasted day. Patrols went here and there to check the possibility of counter attacks; no chance, there was not a German in sight. What we were doing was giving the German High Command that most precious of military advantages: time. Time to organise an aerial counter attack, time to bring up their divisions and time to transport their heavy artillery. We were to lose our advantage and they made us pay — heavily. That evening the Germans opened their offensive. Their aircraft bombed and strafed the beachhead; they sank

HMS *Janus* and badly damaged HMS *Jervis*. Every anti-aircraft gun and most of the Brens pumped shells and bullets into the sky. Streams of tracer wove intricate patterns through which the enemy aeroplanes streaked back home. That was the overture: the first act on the ground was about to begin.

At 7.30 next morning our brigade received orders to advance. About bloody time, we all thought. It had rained incessantly for two days and we were chilled with inactivity. The Grenadiers moved off first. We were on the left flank with the Scots Guards following up in reserve.

So after three days of kicking our heels our commander, Major General Lucas, US Army, finally decided he was ready. The Grenadiers took Aprilia which had been the Fascist party HQ and also a group of buildings which we called 'the Factory', which was dominated by a high square tower which from a distance looked like a chimney stack. This tower was a landmark we all could see, from the beachhead to the Alban Hills. The Irish Guards moved up to the left flank and after slight skirmishing took Carroceto station. Battalion HQ, including yours truly, took over a farmhouse at the rear of an embankment.

The battalion was well established by dusk on 25th January and, apart from occasional shelling and sniping, things were comparatively quiet. As darkness came so did the rain and we spent another cold, soggy night. Dawn came with a heavy hailstorm and we had a wet breakfast. Then the wireless in HQ began to buzz – tanks were rumbling through the morning mist towards the forward positions of No 3 Company. Immediately after this message the heavens opened up and it was not snow that came down. The Germans poured a huge concentration of fire on all the battalion's positions. Guns of all types and calibres opened up on us; there were 150 and 220mm and, for good measure, a monster railway gun which fired a shell that looked like a mini submarine, the only beauty of which was that you could see it coming. I saw one such shell land on a large farmhouse and it completely disintegrated. Luckily it must have taken over an hour to load the damn thing and there were not too many of them. Days later, after it had caused so much damage and casualties, it took an air strike to take it out.

From the high ground round the saucer-like Campo de Carne the Germans could watch every shell land and had the battalion's position pinpointed. Movement was impossible and we dug in like moles. Digging in was easy – not like North Africa where the ground was like rock – but the trouble here was that as soon as you were a couple of feet down, the trench would half fill with water. We cursed the Germans and the stupid sods who had put us here. A batch of German tanks fired two salvos at us and then moved on. With their first salvo they wounded RSM McLoughlin, killed one guardsman and wounded others.

I was desperately sorry for big black McLoughlin; he wished me luck as he trudged to the Regimental Aid Post with blood streaming from his shattered arm. He was dead unlucky. He had broken his ankle on a night exercise just before we left Scotland for North Africa and had rejoined us after the Tunisian campaign and had stood next to me when I was decorated by General Alexander. His ambition was to fight with his own battalion and now he was wounded and out of it. Pain and disappointment were etched on his face.

The morning mist had cleared by now and the enemy had an uninterrupted view of the whole scene. So had we; and our own artillery, after a few ranging rounds, soon saw off the German tanks and the following infantry. No more attacks came in and the enemy concentrated on shelling everything that moved. The long, long day at last came to an end and I think we were all a bit 'bomb happy' at the end of it. We came out of our holes like termites and took advantage of the thickening mist to brew up and have something to eat.

There were fires everywhere. Vehicles, tanks and farm buildings were blazing away merrily, so a few cooking fires would make no odds. The Adjutant was sat by the wireless checking the casualities as they came through; we had lost over 120 men, thirty of whom were dead, mainly caused by shell fire. It had been a bad day.

At dawn the heavy shelling of the previous day was repeated; there were rumours of a heavy American armoured thrust and sure enough a group of American aides turned up looking for somewhere to deploy their tanks. It was pointed out that we were under observation at all times. Notwithstanding this information the Shermans turned up in the afternoon and learned the hard way; they had heavy losses. After the failure of the tank attack it was the turn of the infantry. The Scots and Irish Guards were ordered to take Campoleone Station. It was to be a night attack and we waited anxiously as the reports came in. From the little information that was available it appeared that the battalion reached their objective against heavy opposition but had to withdraw.

That morning I was ordered to collect ammunition from B Echelon in the woods at the back of the beachhead and distribute it amongst the forward companies. I jumped at the opportunity of a bit of action; I was fast becoming disenchanted with my position. It was OK for some to have a 'dug in' job with H.Q. Company but it was not for me. I had been with a rifle company during all my soldiering with the Micks and the constrained regimental life of H.Q. Company did not suit me. I missed the easy comradeship of No 1 Battalion.

Though we were subjected to the same incessant shelling as the forward companies, and very often more so, they at least had the opportunity to hit back. I did not have a 'gung ho' attitude; I simply preferred to take my chance with those I was close to.

On the way to the beachhead I pulled into the courtyard

of a well-kept farm just past Aprilia. It had not suffered much from the shelling — the main signs of which were the dead cattle and pigs which were scattered about. I thought I might be able to scavenge some kit that would be useful to the lads. The previous occupants had left in a hurry — there was stale food on the kitchen table and half of a bottle of wine. Upstairs there was a magnificent double bed with silk sheets; in the wardrobe were a fur coat, evening dresses and drawers packed with silk underwear, both male and female. The place must have belonged to some high-placed Fascist and possibly his mistress; from the erotic pictures on the walls and the fancy underwear, she was certainly no lady. In the cellar were rows of carefully stocked apples and, much to my pleasure, ten bottles of wine and four of cognac. I loaded my loot into the truck and headed for the ammunition dump.

At B Echelon they had run out of Piat bombs and I was advised to pick some up from the beachhead which I approached with trepidation as it was being shelled intermittently by German heavy guns. The beachhead was a hive of activity: boats were being unloaded of their supplies and reloaded with the wounded. I saw lines of German prisoners waiting on the makeshift pier ready to be taken into captivity. Many of them had been press-ganged as stretcher bearers and makeshift dockers. Occasionally all activity would stop as a salvo of shells came over and everybody would dive for cover; luckily most of the shells fell in the sea where there were plenty of wrecked boats and one destroyer, half of which was pointing to the sky. I found the Piat dump, which was run by a company of the Royal West African Regiment. Those black soldiers were very jumpy as they flung cases of bombs onto my truck. I did not blame them: I was jumpy too – one shell on that ammunition dump would have blown us all to Kingdom Come, and half of Italy as well.

Once loaded I left the beachhead like a bat out of hell and made my way back to the forward companies. A sense of foreboding overtook me as I neared the battalion area. There were shell holes everywhere and corpses, both British and German, lying about, abandoned guns and vehicles, some still smouldering, and dead mules and cattle with their hooves in unreal attitudes. There must have been one hell of a fight last night. I found No 1 and No 2 Companies dug in, in the squelchy mud by the side of the sunken road; they had joined forces because of heavy casualties. The lads gathered round me asking what I knew, when were they going to be relieved, were there any reinforcements coming, had I seen the mail truck, how far inland were they . . . I knew nothing. Anzio was like that – nobody ever knew anything. I doled out the wine and apples, and the silk underwear they used to clean the mud off their weapons, which amused everyone. They gave the 'Chief', Sergeant Gundel, the fur coat, which he straight away lined his slit trench with.

I had not been there ten minutes when a battery of .88s

opened up with air bursts. Within seconds I passed from being a good bloke to the worst kind of idiot: the lads reckoned the enemy had spotted my truck and brought the fire down on them. I flopped on top of the fur coat beside Gundel and we cracked open a bottle of cognac while we waited for the shelling to cease. These air bursts were nasty; some of them misfired and we were covered in filth as they flopped into the mud. The shelling soon ended and we gathered round to spin the yarn but not for long – a lengthy burst of Spandau fire raked the muddy embankment in front of us and we dived once again for the trenches. A force of around thirty German infantrymen were dropping into the sunken road from the opposite bank. A short sharp fire fight ensued and we quickly dispatched them whence they came, leaving two dead and three wounded behind them. We suffered two casualties: one guardsman with a shattered knee and another whose ear was creased by a bullet.

The 'Chief' told me that was how it was all the time: a series of short sharp engagements. There was so much cover in the culverts and deep irrigation ditches that the enemy were upon you in seconds and, of course, vice versa when we attacked. I offered to take our two wounded plus the three Germans back with me to the RAP and we gently loaded them onto the truck. Just before I left, Gundel gave me the bad news: my old comrade Bill Pollock, with whom I had shared the same machine-gun burst on the *Bou*, had been killed in the previous night's attack, together with many others of the old No 1 Company guardsmen. This news depressed me: Bill had seemed indestructible and was a big loss. I didn't know if there were even ten guardsmen left of the original company.

I dropped off the remaining ammunition with No 3 HQ who were holed up in a group of identical white farm houses and picked up another guardsman with a broken ankle. I also picked up news I did not want: the latest casualty list. The first name I saw was G. Murphy. Poor Spud had been killed only that morning. He and his whole section had walked into doubled back machine guns and had been cut in half. He was the type of guardsman that was irreplaceable. His face and form are still very clear to me after all these years. He was a superb young man. At least he had had some pleasure and fun in our interlude at Castellammare.

It had been a bad day. Worse was to come for the battalions of the 24th Guards Brigade. The long-predicted German counter-attack erupted in early February. The heavy enemy guns on the slopes of the Alban Hills opened up. It was easy to see by their number and intensity of fire that this was to be a great offensive. The eruption of smoke and flying earth around the 'Factory' showed where the main attack was to be aimed. The heavy shelling paused; the enemy tanks advanced, rattling and clanging, followed by the infantry. Every piece of artillery was targeted on this narrow front. Some of our heavy guns were backed into the sea to enable them to drop their range to hit the new targets. Again and again the enemy attacked, suffering staggering casualties in the process. The German infantry advancing across the open ground were driven back. Again and again they came on. In spite of the bitterest resistance of the Anzio campaign, by the end of the day a huge gap had been carved out of the Allied line.

The battalions of the 24th Guards Brigade were called forward to take up a last-ditch position barring the exit of the main road but the heroic resistance of the 1st Loyals and the 2nd Battalion of the US 157th combat team held off the Germans – just. Crisis was reached by the second night of the offensive. Attack after attack was mounted by the persistent Germans: they all but got through, but then even they called time. The slaughter and casualties on both sides had been tremendous. As dawn broke the attacks ceased and the gunfire simmered down. Both sides needed time to collect their dead and wounded, time to regroup and count the cost. In hindsight it is now possible to see that this was the vital action and the beachhead was now safe; however, none of us present on that warm spring morning realised these facts at the time.

The battalion had had three days and four nights of vicious close-quarter fighting, very similar to the fighting we had experienced on the *Bou* in North Africa. Each enemy attack was followed by another, pressed home with grim German determination – to be met with equally grim aggressive defence, since the spirit and comradeship of the Irish Guards was as usual of the highest order. Many of my friends distinguished themselves in these actions; the Chief, Sergeant Clem Gundel, won a DCM (not before time). He was a morose character and his pessimism knew no limits; he regarded the antics of his Irish soldiers with bored toleration. He was the classic English soldier, dour and determined; if he was ordered to stick, he stuck, and the whole German army would not move him. It was my privilege and honour to serve with him. Two of my comrades from No 1 Company were awarded DCMs: 'Hopper' Adamson and 'Monty' Montgomery – two very fine guardsmen who became legends in the regiment. These two were very like myself: 'chancers' who risked their luck. The phlegmatic Guardsman Ryan picked up a well-deserved MM for collecting many wounded under heavy fire.

Drill Sergeant Kenny was now acting RSM and he detailed me and another guardsman to go down to the beachhead and pick up any reinforcements if they had arrived; we were very short of men and they were coming in dribs and drabs. Indeed, the guardsman with me had only arrived on a mixed transport the day before, but the poor guy was not to live long. As I rounded the bend on the bumpy track that led to the main Anzio road there was a loud crack and the guardsman slumped across me. I swerved into a ditch, managed to pull onto the track and stopped fifty yards on. He was stone dead, shot through the neck; the bullet had shattered his spinal cord and he was killed instantly. I was soaked with his blood. I got out and dragged him from the passenger seat and laid him in the ditch. I took off his ID discs and went through his pockets to see if he had any possessions I could hand on; he had very little: infantry soldiers are almost always poor. As I laid him out there was a sharp crack and a hiss and another bullet ploughed into his left leg. 'Christ,' I thought, 'it's a sniper, he's after me,' and I dived under the truck. He could not get a clear shot at me under there.

I gathered my thoughts as I cowered under the Bedford; he must be on my left: the first shot had killed my passenger, we had rounded a bend and travelled some fifty yards before stopping, and the second shot had come when I'd dragged the poor guy out, again on the left; he could not shoot round bends so he must obviously be up high. I peered cautiously from under the rear wheels. There was the cover, about 250 yards on my left, a large group of pine trees, tall and thick with foliage. The bastard must be in there somewhere. I realised that from his angle of view all he could see was the back of the truck and the passenger side; I could crawl under the truck, into the driver's seat, start up and be away. I thought again. The moment I started the motor it would alert him and he would have time to pump three or four shots through the back of the truck before I could get into gear. I could not chance it. I had to try and take him out. I was working myself up into a cold fury. This was bloody guerrilla war; every soldier hates snipers: the odds are always with them. It was to be him or me.

I crawled under the truck and managed to remove the Bren gun from under the driver's seat. So far, so good. Beyond the ditch where I had laid the guardsman was a deep irrigation gully which followed the line of the track and round the bend. I judged it about ten yards from the front of the truck. If I could make that, I would have cover almost to the line of the trees. Should I crawl those ten yards and hope he did not spot me, or run it? Shit or bust I curled myself like a spring and dived for the gully; he got off one shot and missed by a mile. I reckon I covered those ten yards in less than a second; self preservation makes supermen of us all. I landed in the gully, which must have been a foot deep in mud and filth. I wrapped my field dressing round the breech and mechanism of the Bren — this was no time for slip-ups — and crawled well over a hundred yards down the gully till it petered out into a culvert which was covered with undergrowth. By this time I was well camouflaged myself, being covered in mud. I worked my way slowly through the undergrowth to the top of the culvert and peered anxiously through it. I was no more than seventy yards from the trees; all I had to do was spot him.

I slid the Bren gun forward and planted its legs firmly in the earth and got behind it. Where was the bastard? I searched and scanned those trees till my eyes almost popped out. Not a sign. There were occasional movements and rustling but it was only birds. I did not expect the glint of a rifle barrel. These snipers were too clever for that: they were always covered. I watched endlessly, but nothing; the adrenalin had gone away by now and I thought he must have moved away. I considered heading back for the truck and taking my chance. Suddenly, to my right and high in the dense trees, I saw the slightest of gleams; he must have moved fractionally and the sun caught the end of his telescopic sight. I pin-pointed the spot and eased the gun into my shoulder. I blasted the whole magazine off into the trees. The noise was shattering after the silence. I put the butt down and watched and waited. The birds had all scattered away, squawking their heads off; then I heard a loud rustling in the trees. There he was, dropping through the foliage from branch to branch till he ended up in a crumpled heap in the long grass. I'd got him and I felt great.

I sprinted over the ground and straightened him out. That long burst had all but taken his head off; he had no jaw and his face was a bloody mess. He must have been dead well before he hit the ground. I ripped open his camouflage jacket; he was a corporal in the Panzer Grenadiers; he had pictures of himself standing on the steps of the Acropolis in Greece and various snaps of himself with different girl friends; he must have been a Romeo. I threw his wallet away; it was no use to me. I took his wrist watch though:

it was Swiss and looked very expensive; it was not to bring me much luck.

I debated whether to return to battalion HQ or carry on, and decided to go to the beachhead. I turned off the track onto the main road and ran into more slaughter. I heard shell fire and presumed they were having a go at the beachhead, but I was wrong. The enemy guns were concentrating on a transport convoy spread over about half a mile. The occasional truck would be blown high in the air and one exploded like a giant sparkler. Telephone poles were snapping like matchsticks, wires were snaking across the road; a nearby house received a direct hit and split down the middle, each side dropping into dust and rubble. I pulled up behind an RAMC ambulance; it was impossible to leave the road as there were muddy ditches to each side. The enemy guns dropped their range a little and shells were falling all around us; this was no place to be so I baled out of the truck into the nearby ditch. There was a stench of cordite from the explosions; the fumes grabbed at my throat and made me retch.

On the other side of the road was a typical Italian cemetery packed with headstones and fancy monuments with angels and cherubs flying around – a very apt place, I thought. What interested me more was that one side of the cemetery was built into a cliff face with graves let into it and covered with metal plates. Built into the end of the cliff was a substantial looking type of lodge; that was the place to be. I listened carefully – no shells – and made a dive for it. Inside was a middle-aged corporal of the RAMC with his driver, who had obviously had the same idea as me. 'Are you alright?' the Corporal said. 'I'm fine,' I replied. 'Good. I've got four people in the ambulance, three of them stretcher cases. Will you help us get them out before the whole bloody road is blown up?'

The shelling ceased for a time and we got them into the lodge plus some blankets and canvas bags of First Aid kit. The corporal had some very strange patients – one was a terrified, heavily pregnant Italian girl of about eighteen with a thigh wound, accompanied by an elderly woman who was in a state of shock; the other two were from the 'Loyals' – one a sergeant who had a smashed kneecap, the other a private who had lost half his foot; they had gone over a mine. The sergeant was very stoic; the private, who looked no older than the girl, was delirious with pain and shock and wanted his mother. The corporal knew his kit and gave the two soldiers a shot of morphine each from the plastic capsules we used to carry. The young soldier quietened down but the girl was a different kettle of fish. The corporal was worried that the state of shock she was in would bring on a premature birth; the old woman was less than useless, telling her beads and begging the saints to save her.

The shelling started again and some exploded in the cemetery itself; earth, stones and lumps of masonry rattled on the roof of the lodge. The roof was very thick and we were in no danger unless we had a direct hit but the noise and stench started the old woman off again and terrified the girl. When the shelling ceased for a while I took a look outside. It was a scene of horror; some of the graves had been blown apart and there were bones everywhere, bits of flesh and arms and legs from the recently buried were lying on flattened gravestones. The stench was appalling – it gave me the creeps. The metal plates covering the graves let into the cliff side had been blown off. These graves must have been a couple of centuries old; all that remained of their occupants were skeletons, some with rings still on the finger bones; I noticed that the fallen hair had retained its colour.

The corporal was right: the last barrage had done for the girl and she was in labour. He was absolutely brilliant; he delivered that child, a boy, perfectly and after the horrors I had just seen it lifted my soul as he cleaned up the new-born child and it started to cry. He deserved my Victoria Cross and lots more like it; he was a great human being and probably got nothing but the thanks of the young mother. He made me feel very humble.

This was an occasion and time for a drink. I had nearly a full bottle of my precious cognac in the truck and I nipped outside to retrieve it. A shell must have landed near the ambulance; its doors were blown off, my truck was lying on its side, and petrol was seeping all over the road. I'd wrapped the booze in my greatcoat, and luckily it was intact. Then my proverbial luck ran out.

I'd heard the shell coming and judged it to be going over. I was wrong and over confident; it landed about thirty yards away among the gravestones. I felt a sharp stinging pain in my right wrist. 'Jesus Christ,' I thought, 'I've been hit,' and dived for the safety of the lodge. The corporal removed the shrapnel that was sticking out from the inside of my wrist – only it was not shrapnel, it was silver grey marble from one of the memorial stones. He poured some of the cognac, which sensibly I had not dropped, over the wound and sprinkled it with the usual sulpha-adamide powder and put on a field dressing. We all had a drink and I needed one. The old woman had regained her composure and was cleaning the young mother up as best she could, the wounded Loyals were coming round from the morphine injections and the new addition to our makeshift family was in his mother's arms.

We reviewed the situation. My wrist was throbbing painfully, the field dressing was soaked in blood and it was dripping from my fingers. He had another look at it and said the artery in the wrist had probably been nicked; he put a tourniquet on my upper arm and a sling to hold the wrist high. The decision was made for us. I had to get to the Forward dressing station. It was imperative for the soldiers and the girl to get medical attention. Leaving the corporal to tend to his charges the medical orderly and I headed down the road. Happily the shelling had ceased and the transport guys had started to clear the road. We made the dressing station and I wished the orderly luck as he went to make arrangements to pick up the corporal and his charges. They were good guys and a credit to the RAMC.

The doctor replaced my dressings and changed the tourniquet for pressure pads but I was still losing blood. He gave me an injection of I know not what and I was sent down to the casualty clearing station. Conditions here were chaotic due to the recent heavy shelling; the wounded were teeming in and there was no time for niceties. The dead were laid in rows on the ground, the stretchers were needed for the wounded. Emergency operations were being carried out in various tents; arms and legs, some with a boot still on, were thrown outside – it was a place of the utmost horror. A blood-stained surgeon had a look at me. Although it was a small wound, the artery was damaged and I had lost a lot of blood. I was to be evacuated, and a label was slapped on me.

Outside the tent I saw CSM Mercer on a stretcher; he had been brought in by CSM Pestell. He had a wound in the thigh that you could put your fist in; he was terrified that they would take his leg off. Happily for Mercer they did not and he went on to gain high rank in the regiment. I was evacuated and given another injection on the boat. I was feeling very low and depressed and, what with fatigue and loss of blood, plus the recent injection, I passed out. I woke in the 60th General Naples; the Italian campaign was over for me.

I was quite ill for a couple of weeks but began to pick up on my third week. From newly arrived guardsmen I learned that the battalion had suffered so many casualties that they were to be relieved and taken out of Anzio. This was good news – the battalion had done its share and it was not before time.

On 6th March a new brigade landed and the orders were reissued. Major General P. Penney, CBE, DSO, MC went to say goodbye to the battalion. 'I can't let you go without saying how much I shall miss the Regiment not only collectively, but individually. It has been a privilege and a sadness to have had your battalion in the 1st Division during these days, but their achievements, their unfailing response and their willing fighting spirit have been an inspiration. I regret your departure enormously, especially as I fear there is little chance of your rejoining us, but I am glad of the opportunity you will have for refitting and reforming. I wish you all well, and I shall never forget what you have done and the sacrifices you have made.' The battalion sailed from Anzio on 7th March 1944 – it was a beautiful morning.

It was a beautiful morning for me too, for who should come walking through the wards but a young Irish Guards subaltern who was checking on the members of his regiment. It sharply reminded me of what a family regiment the Irish Guards were; no matter which theatre of war they were in, every effort was made to account for each guardsman, rich or poor. This concern went on into civilian life and many ex-guardsmen have reason to thank the regiment. I had a quick word with the officer; those of us on the mend would be posted to a convalescent camp near Sorrento where the rest of the battalion were going for rest and rehabilitation.

Slowly the remnants of the battalion began to gather at Sorrento. The wounded had been in hospitals all over southern Italy, some even in Sicily. We convalesced together including the survivors of the beachhead who really needed rest. Even after the battles in North Africa, seldom had I seen the soldiers so gaunt and shattered. Adding to the general feeling of depression within the unit, Vesuvius erupted.

White-hot streams of lava poured from the crater, the grey dust turned day into night, the roads were blocked and the beautiful hills and green valleys evolved into a dull grey desert landscape. The dust got everywhere and it was difficult to breathe. The earth trembled with each eruption and it was as if the world was coming to an end. One wag remarked that Hitler had dropped a bloody great bomb into the crater to trigger it and finally finish us off; some believed him. The eruptions petered out after a couple of days and we started to pull ourselves together. Then the news came through; there were no more Irish Guards reinforcements in this theatre of war.

The 1st Battalion was finished as a fighting unit. We were to prepare for embarkation and hand over all our weapons and equipment. We were going home. Just before we left, our Commanding Officer, Colonel Scott, was promoted Brigadier and joined the 8th Army. We were all sorry to see him go; without question he was one of the great wartime battalion commanders and it was a great pity that he, who had led us through so much, could not take us home.

On 11th April the battalion sailed from Naples in the *Capetown Castle*. Of the 926 men who left Ayr in February 1943, 326 landed in Liverpool on 22nd April 1944. On the beachhead the battalion had lost 32 officers and 714 men, killed, wounded and missing. These figures tell their own story and the 1st Battalion never fought again as a single unit. We landed at Liverpool to a low-key welcome from phlegmatic and disinterested dockers. We were quickly put on a train for London and coaches took us to Chelsea Barracks. After the beauty of the Sorrento peninsula, war-torn Britain looked old and tired – a little like ourselves.

CHAPTER 10

TIDYING UP

We had a hectic week at Chelsea before going on leave. All of us were fully kitted out and our battledresses were tailored to make us look like guardsmen again. Most of us had lost everything on the beachhead. I had lost all the letters I had kept and the souvenirs that I had picked up here and there; even Maria's gold medallion had gone. The only thing left to me was the sniper's watch, which served me for many years. One thing we did have was plenty of money, as we were paid for the first time in a long time. Money – I had not given it a thought for ages. An infantry soldier's wealth is his courage, loyalty, steadfastness under fire, his comradeship and love for his fellow soldiers. Shattering experiences shared are of greater value than all of Croesus' wealth; a bullet does not know or care if you are a millionaire or not.

During that hectic week we all had thorough medical examinations; I came out class 'A': fit for active duty. Some of the guys were downgraded, including my old friend, 'The Chief'. I was pleased for him; it meant he would survive the war and take his miserable self back to his wife and son. No man had done more for his country than him. Inevitably during that week, word got round that the Irish Guards were back from the war and I suddenly found myself a celebrity. War-weary Britain was looking for heroes and I found myself a 'pop star' of my generation. There were invitations for this, that and the other, press reporters wanted interviews and lots of mail came in. It was much too early for me; I did not want to know. All I wanted was to retreat behind the anonymity of an ordinary Irish Guardsman. I was only just twenty-three, I badly needed sound advice and there was no one to guide me.

There was one particular call on my time that I was duty bound to attend to; there were frequent callers at the barrack gate, usually mothers, wives and sweethearts of guardsmen killed or missing in action, enquiring what I knew of their loved ones. 'Did I know him?' 'Was I near him at the time?' And the eternal question, 'Did he die quickly and not suffer?' Their grief was so personal they naturally assumed that I knew them, which of course in many cases I did not, but I was a name and a guardsman like their loved one and someone who they could relate to and ask. Where I could help, I hope that I did and where I could not I made enquiries of other soldiers and passed on what information I could. All in all these occasions were quite traumatic.

A lesson that I learned quickly was that I would have to put on a different front. As a living holder of the Victoria Cross, I was a mirror of my regiment; it was harder wearing the medal than winning it. The hectic week fled by and I was glad that the whole battalion was going on a fortnight's leave. It would be good to have some peace and quiet – get away from all the hoo-ha and put my own life in some sort of order. I would get to know my young wife whom I had hardly spent any time with and whom I had almost forgotten in the events of the past year.

I had phoned my wife to let her know which train I was on. As we approached my stop, which was Dudley Port, there were few people left on the train. The train guard approached me and said, 'Is your name Kenneally the VC?' I nodded and he shook my hand. 'There's a brass band and hundreds of people waiting to see you at the station.' I cursed under my breath; that was the last thing I wanted. Tipton, Staffs, was a small industrial Black Country town wrapped up in its war effort; every factory was churning out ammunition or guns. Although I was not 'of them', they made me an adopted son and attempted to use me in encouraging those efforts.

The welcoming brass band was just a start. Invitations flooded in; would I attend a Home Guard dinner? Would I go to this dance or that function? Would I open a local fete? Would I praise the local war effort from the stage of the local Hippodrome? The local papers were full of me and followed me about; I went along with it for a few days, because I did feel I had a duty and the people were genuine. There were one or two amusing incidents. One local paper headlined me as the famous 'English' Guardsman; I thought the Regimental Lieutenant Colonel would love that – my shoulder flashes were obvious enough. I attended a local dance in aid of something or other and met the Countess of Dudley; she was as bored as I, doing her duty much as I was.

I'd had enough. I could not go out for a quiet drink without being asked: 'What did you do to win a Victoria Cross?' It was a question I grew to hate. I got a local tailor to make me a new civilian suit, no coupons; it is amazing how a little notoriety greases the wheels. It was the answer: I did get a drink in peace. I had promised to open a fete in the local park on the Saturday afternoon. I turned up in my new suit. 'Where's your uniform?' the Mayor asked me. 'We wanted a soldier to open the fete.' I spotted a private in the North Staffs Regiment standing at the front of the taped-off rostrum. 'Get him to open your fete,' I said. 'He's a soldier just like me, and he's from your local regiment.' 'But he's got no medal,' the Mayor remonstrated. That remark showed me a lot; the local bigwigs never regarded me in quite the same light after that incident. I opened the fete to loud cheers and it went off well.

A mood of deep depression filled me for the remainder of my leave. I do not know what caused it – perhaps it was a reaction to what had gone before. I was glad to return to Chelsea. As soon as I saw the guardsmen cutting about the barrack square the mood lifted; it was good to be back with people I could understand. I'd had enough of civilian life.

May 1944 was to be a busy time. An investiture was being

organised for honours and awards to be presented by His Majesty King George VI at Buckingham Palace. We were also to be inspected by the Regimental Lieutenant Colonel, affectionately or otherwise known as 'Black Fitz'. More importantly, the future of the 1st Battalion was to be discussed.

Extra drill was the order of the day, stricter discipline was imposed, past glories were to be forgotten; we were guardsmen and the Drill Sergeants made sure we did not forget it. The investiture was fixed for the day after the Regimental Lieutenant Colonel's inspection.

An hour before his parade 'Black Fitz' sent for me. He was a martinet of the old school; he had served in the First World War with distinction and was a man of high morals. Honour, duty and integrity were his watchwords. He was a hard disciplinarian but fair. I am sure he thought all young guardsmen were natural scoundrels and had to be moulded and disciplined into his way. 'You can leave us Drill Sergeant,' he said to Drill Sgt. Kenny who had marched me in. 'I will speak to Sergeant Kenneally alone.' 'Oh dear,' I thought, 'has he found out all about me?'

He looked at me for a full minute and then said, 'I have been going through your records, Kenneally, and though bearable they are not all they should be. You realise that once His Majesty pins that Victoria Cross on you tomorrow you will become a living legend of the Irish Guards, an example of the Regiment and someone future guardsmen will learn about and look up to. From now on I want your behaviour to be exemplary, is that understood?'

I thought on my feet. 'Should I stop this before it starts; should I tell him that I was not what I seemed; that my name was not Kenneally but Jackson and I don't know where it came from; that I was not an Irishman but half English and half Jew; that I had deserted the Royal Artillery to join the regiment? Why should I?'

It did not matter whether I was black, white or yellow – I was an Irish Guardsman. It did not matter whether my name was Smith, Cohen or Kelly – I was an Irish Guardsman. They had seen fit to give me the medal; I had not asked for it. I was just as proud and honoured to be a member of the regiment as he was; and anyway, if I told the old bugger all this I might give him a heart attack.

I nodded and answered, 'I understand, Sir, and will do my best to be a credit to the Regiment.' This was the answer he wanted and his manner visibly softened towards me. 'I have been considering posting you to the Guards Depot,' he said. 'You can help train the new recruits; that will give you a good background. This war will not last much longer and you will have a great future in the Regiment. What have you to say to that?'

That was the last thing I wanted – the Guards Depot: all that bullshit. I pointed out that I was only twenty-three and had just passed the medical A1 and fit for active service. I would very much like to stay with the battalion in a rifle company and be a duty soldier. If I was lucky enough to survive the war then I would think about signing on for a further period of service. 'As you wish,' he said, and wished me luck. 'We will talk again in the future.' I liked and respected him; for all his stiff and formal manner, he was probably one of the last of the old type of Guards Officers.

The big day of the investiture arrived and it was to be the largest of that year; for that very reason each recipient was limited to one guest. I took my wife. This decision was to cause a permanent and unsurmountable rift between my mother and my wife.

My mother had met my wife only briefly, two days before we married, and was not impressed. 'What do you want to marry her for?' she said. 'You're too young, she's older than you. On top of that, she's Welsh and I know those Welsh women. Marry her if you must, but it won't last and in any case I'm not coming to the wedding.' She didn't; hardly a good start to their relationship. The two women were as different as chalk and cheese and although it is a dangerous thing to say about women, I understood both of them; there was good and bad on both sides. My mother, as I have said before, was of good family and well educated and had a bright future until her liaison with my father. From then on for some years it had been downhill for her and, of course, for the appendage with her: me. In her days, in the depressed years before the war, she had been a lady of no great virtue; in those tough days she had fed and clothed me and got me a good education, and she had tried to keep her values. We know she was a snob and loved the good things of life; she liked to party, to drink and smoke and much preferred the company of men. I had been a disappointment to her going in the army: the RAF or even the navy were much more respectable. However, through all my ups and downs she had supported me; when I won the medal she was very proud of me. All the slights and sneers she suffered through having an illegitimate son were washed away. She had produced a boy who had won a Victoria Cross; her nose was higher than ever. Such was my mother.

My wife was a very different type of woman. Tragically orphaned at fourteen, she had been brought up by her older sister in the strict Welsh methodist pattern of her parents. Her moral education had been of the highest order; she had been raised by women who believed men were only after one thing and that marriage was the only bedrock a girl could rely on. She was tall, beautiful with a great figure, rather shy. The moment I had seen her at the dance hall in Birmingham I knew she was very different to the short-time girls I was used to. The Yanks were taking all the pretty girls at that time but they did not take this one. Years after, she admitted to me that she used to go to the Birmingham dances hoping she would meet a young man who would take her out of the humdrum life of the Black Country. What she saw in me I will never know, but I certainly livened her life up for her. She insisted on marriage and marriage is what she got. I was as kind to her as I possibly could be, and she gave herself to me utterly and completely. The cynicism was wiped out of my mind: she really loved me, she really did. Such was my wife.

I explained my dilemma about who to bring to the investiture to my wife. There were no tantrums from her; she was of the old school who believed the husband's word was law.

'You must decide what's best.' she said, 'she's your mother. I'm easy either way.' Almost as an aside she quietly said, 'Still, if we are lucky enough to have children it would be nice to tell them that I was with their father when he was decorated by the King.' She had won hands down, and she knew it. I caught the smug little smile under her lowered eyes as she said it. Oh, how devious women can be! (We did later have two sons together and she took great pride in showing them pictures of the two of us at Buckingham Palace.) My mother was very miffed with this decision and never forgave 'the Black Country woman', as she called her, for taking what she thought was her rightful place at the ceremony.

All the recipients gathered in the courtyard of the palace with their guests. It was a fine sunny day, a good day for dying as foot soldiers would say, but a better day to get a medal. Sergeant Gundel and I introduced each other's wives and they palled up together. The guests were ushered into the massive gilded Throne Room and sat on red plush chairs at the rear; above them in the balcony the band of the

Grenadier Guards played light chamber music. They were each given a programme of events by the numerous footmen and equerries who were scurrying about.

The recipients were placed in a side room and were all told the drill; what we had to do, and in what order and number. Each medal recipient had a small metal hook placed over his left breast pocket, the reason for this being obvious. A very toffee-nosed equerry checked us out individually and told us in what order we were to go in and meet the King. We were to walk in quietly; no caps or hats to be worn so no saluting. We were to go in order of precedence. I was to be the first, the Victoria Cross holding precedence over all the other honours and awards; then would come the various orders, then the knighthoods, baronets, etc; then the military decorations, DSO, MC, etc., and the other ranks DCMs, MMs and the equivalent decorations for the other services, and finally the civilian awards, MBEs, etc.

The band struck up the National Anthem. The King entered from a small side door. The Master of Ceremonies announced His Majesty King George VI of Great Britain and the British Empire, Emperor of India, Defender of the Faith, etc; he seemed to go on for half an hour. He paused and then said, 'His Majesty had graciously awarded the Victoria Cross to Sergeant John Patrick Kenneally of the 1st Battalion Irish Guards': that was my cue. I took a deep breath and out I walked to face the King. The Master of

Ceremonies carried on reading my citation, the King took the medal from a purple cushion that was handed to him and hung it from the hook on my chest; we shook hands and he congratulated me. He was a much smaller man than I had imagined and was dressed in Naval uniform. He asked me if I was fit and well after my wounds. I said I was. He mentioned that he had visited the battalion at Ayr before we went abroad; had I been there? I said I had. With a light stammer he said that he had very much enjoyed the day.

That was it. I turned to the left and walked out of the Throne Room into an ante-room where an equerry took the medal, placed it in a satin-lined box and directed me to the guests' seats, where I sat between Mrs Gundel and my wife. It was all over and I settled down to watch the rest of the proceedings. I was certainly in the company of captains and kings. I watched naval commanders, barons, generals and air marshals getting the Order of this, that and the other, and soldiers, sailors and airmen getting their medals. It was all carried out with great pomp and circumstance; it was what the British Empire was all about.

After the ceremony we gathered in the courtyard. The newsreel men, reporters and photographers descended on us; some of the lads from the regiment had gathered outside the gates and gave us a big cheer. We insisted on having photographs taken with them. It was an extraordinary occasion and a good day for the Micks.

*　　*　　*

Whilst the 1st Battalion had been on its travels abroad, the 2nd and 3rd Battalions had been training with the Guards Armoured Division, the 2nd being equipped with Sherman and Firefly tanks and the 3rd established as motorised infantry. This was the first time ever that foot guards had been put into tanks; it was a one-off ploy for the thrust into Europe and right well were they to do it.

The church bells rang in June of 1944, heralding the invasion. Our 2nd and 3rd Battalions landed in Normandy at Arromanches towards the end of the month. Very few veterans of the African and Italian campaigns were used in the initial invasion of Europe; they were mostly untried officers and men — sometimes it is better not to know what you are in for. When, some time later, I saw the German defences on the Normandy beachheads I was very thankful I was not of the brave number who first attacked them. In the safety of the Sergeants' Mess in the Chelsea barracks we raised our glasses and wished the lads well.

I had a good friend of long standing in the 2nd Battalion called Mahon. We had been recruits together at the Guards Depot; his number was 2722931, mine 2722925, so there was not much between us in service. His father was one time Lord Mayor of Bootle near Liverpool; he was an introspective, well-educated lad, a cut above the usual wisecracking macho Liverpudlian types. He had a hard time in our early months at the Guards Depot and training battalion. He hated the discipline and bullshit of the Brigade and was one of those unfortunate guys who could never get the knack of looking after his kit – fatal for a guardsman; he was often in trouble and easy prey for the more asinine non-coms. I had palled up with him and helped him along the way as much as I could; I liked him and we would have long talks and arguments that were way, way above the usual guardsman's patter of wine, women and song.

After I had been posted to the 1st Battalion and gone abroad he corresponded with me regularly. He was given the opportunity of joining the 2nd Battalion and training in armoured warfare. He had jumped at the chance – anything to get away from the eternal drill, route marches and weapon training which he hated. I had the usual infantryman's dislike of tanks and told him so; to me, tanks meant only one thing – trouble. I found them claustrophobic and much preferred to be on my own two feet; he would argue that being inside a tank was much safer and the chance of survival greater. That theory to me was questionable.

His squadron was among the first of the Irish Guards to go into action in Normandy. Completely outgunned by a German Panther, his tank was blown to pieces. I read his name on the first casualty list; there it was: 2722931 Guardsman Mahon, killed in action. It was a sad shock. Two days after the casualty list appeared I received a letter from him; it must have been among the last he wrote. In it he said that tank crews lived in the lap of luxury by infantry standards: they carried their own water and petrol stoves and that they all shaved most days; the biggest hazard was the choking dust kicked up by the tank tracks.

He told me about an amusing incident involving a Normandy farmer. The Sherman was overheating and they turned off the road towards a farm to take on more water. In the farm courtyard, out of courtesy, they asked the grizzled Norman farmer for water. No doubt angered by the way the tank had churned up his farm track, he refused. Mahon told me these Normans were a law unto themselves; they were not Frenchmen but Normans and it was not their war. They were heartily sick of the French, the Germans and now here were the British demanding things of them. He was short of water for his own cattle and the well was low – in fact, empty. The lieutenant commanding the tank was having none of this. He again asked politely for water. If the farmer did not comply with his request he would be forced to blow his roof off with the big gun on the tank. The Norman just shrugged his shoulders; he thought the officer was bluffing. But he wasn't. He gave the necessary orders and the gunner put an armour-piercing shell through the bedroom window and out through the roof. The farmer rapidly produced a rope and bucket and the water was soon forthcoming; not everyone wanted to be liberated, said Mahon.

Tragically, he must have been killed a couple of days after this incident. Sadly I put away his letter; although disillusioned by the role of a guardsman he could do no more for the regiment than give his life to it. He was one of the first of the many casualties suffered by the 2nd and 3rd Battalions in Normandy and this obviously was to have its effect on the remnants of the 1st Battalion. The junketing in London was over and we were sent to Scotland to train as motorised infantry and later to be sent as reinforcements to the 3rd Battalion.

Stobbs Camp, Hawick, was our destination and our home for some months. Hawick was a beautiful Scottish border town famous for its woollens; what sticks in my memory was the first time I ever saw mirrors set in the walls each side of the upper windows so that the old people could sit and watch who was coming up and down the street. The local girls welcomed the 'Micks' with open arms as did the WAAFs from the nearby RAF station. There were many whirlwind romances and indeed I attended the wedding of an old friend, Sergeant Gerry Phelan, and his young bride Anne. Forty years and many children later I met them both again in North Africa; this was one wartime marriage that lasted. The last bastion in southern Italy, Monte Cassino, fell, our old comrades on the Anzio beachhead broke out and Yankee General Mark Clark realised his ambition of driving into Rome.

General Alexander, who had overall command, was made a Field Marshal and given the title Earl of Tunis. He was also given the Freedom of the City of London and I was invited to attend the ceremony at the Guildhall as the representative of the Regiment. It was a truly magnificent occasion with even more pomp and circumstance than I had seen at the Palace. All the establishment were seated round the sides of the Guildhall: members of the Government, Dukes and Duchesses, Lords and Ladies, Admirals, Generals, Air Marshals and representatives of all nations. I was stood at the back with a small group of soldiers. The trumpeters of the Household Brigade blasted off and then the Master of Ceremonies gave out each of our names and individual regiments; we then walked individually through the applauding peers and were ushered to seats right at the front. It was a nice touch: Alexander had not forgotten that it was the poor bloody infantry that had got him there.

Back at the ranch the 1st Battalion was no more. We were reorganised into one Company named 'No 4' and were due to go to France as a complete entity and join the 3rd Battalion to replace 'X' Company Scots Guards. We were looking forward to it. It may seem strange that men would want to go back into action but it is a fact. You can have too much training and regimental discipline; we were young and every man jack amongst us felt a touch of guilt as we read the casualty list: we should be there with the regiment and our comrades. At the last moment senior NCOs on the draft were withdrawn from it. They had an important job for us. We were sick as pigs as the guardsmen marched off. Among them were two pals of mine: we had been recruits together – McGarry and Rafferty from Runcorn. They both had come through Africa and Italy without a scratch and I hoped their luck would continue.

Happily, when I rejoined the company a few months later in Germany when the hostilities were nearly over, there at the right of the line was big McGarry and further down the ranks I saw the rugged English face of Rafferty. They had made it and I was very pleased – they were the very stuff of the regiment. The British 2nd Army had broken out of Normandy and were heading for Belgium and Holland; the cost had been high and they were very short of reinforcements, especially infantry. The powers-that-be were scraping the barrel; all supernumeraries and men under twenty-five in the RAF who were surplus to requirements were to be transferred to the Army and trained as infantrymen. The squadron commanders in the RAF rubbed their hands; this was a heaven-sent opportunity to get rid of all their scroungers and malingerers, those with bad records and those they did not like. It was to be our job to train them as soldiers and to turn them into guardsmen.

The convoy of trucks spilled out the reluctant RAF men on to the barrack square. They had already been documented and allocated, the majority going to the Grenadiers and Coldstreams; the Irish Guards ended up with about eighty. These were divided into three squads with a squad instructor, a Lance sergeant, a corporal and a couple of trained soldiers to help him; I was a squad instructor. Drill Sergeant Kenny took charge of proceedings and it was an education to see how his years of experience in dealing with recalcitrant soldiers were brought into play. He could have bounced them with the shock horror tactics of the Guards Depot; instead, he spoke to them quietly and said he realised that they had been transferred to the army not by their own free will but by the dictates of war; they were fortunate, however, to be instructed in their new role by the finest soldiers in the British Army. As he introduced us to our charges he told them they had probably never seen Irish Guardsmen on a Drill Parade and so he put all of us in one square to give them a demonstration.

It was twenty minutes of pure Guards magic. There is nothing the Micks like better than putting on a show. We wheeled and turned, marched in quick and slow time, sloped, ordered and presented arms, fixed and unfixed bayonets with cool professionalism. We might be the 'Pongos' or brown jobs as they called us but we were proud men and it showed. Kenny halted us with a satisfied nod and dismissed us to our squads. He told them if they approached that standard in the next ten to twelve weeks they would be allowed to wear the eight-pointed star and put up their Irish Guards shoulder flashes.

It was not easy. These guys had some military training as they all had eight weeks of it on their induction into the RAF. In some ways it would have been better if they had none; they had picked up so many bad habits. We drilled and demonstrated, then more drill, hours of PT, then more drill.

After the first week I lost six of my squad: two went over the wall and four failed the medical. However, with the loss of those men we also lost the biggest proportion of the real bad hats and barrack room lawyers. Slowly, very slowly, they began to get the hang of things and learned how we operated in the Brigade of Guards. They began gradually to improve. With the introduction of inter-squad and inter-regimental competitions they improved further and began to ask questions about their training and the regiment. This was a good sign; whereas before they would listen sullenly, now they were taking an interest.

The experiment of transforming aircraftmen into infantry soldiers succeeded and by the end of that year they passed out as guardsmen. My squad came second out of the whole intake in drill and elementary weapon training.

As each squad passed out, their training completed, they were packed off to Europe to reinforce the 3rd Battalion. No man went until he was proficient in arms and could look after himself; the country was scraping the barrel for fighting soldiers at that time and the Brigade of Guards should be justifiably proud of the way these ex-RAF men were turned into competent guardsmen. In subsequent actions they committed themselves well and some were killed and wounded. One of my original squad, who had been the most obstreperous in learning his new trade, won a Military Medal for gallantry.

During this period of training I was invited to various social events. One I attended was a local WVS dance at Lingfield where I was asked to present the 'Sport' prizes. Arriving late with an old chum of mine, Sgt Dolan, we stood at the back of the hall watching proceedings. In front of us stood a couple of guys from the RASC; one said to the other: 'An Irish Guards VC is going to dish out the prizes tonight.' 'Oh yes,' said his mate, 'where is he?' 'I dunno,' his mate replied, 'have a look round. He's sure to have a light on it.' 'Shall I put him right?' said Frank Dolan. 'Don't bother,' I replied. The British love to knock their heroes.

About this time the Royal Navy had turned the tide against the German U-boats and many were limping into the Southern Irish ports where they were getting succour and help. The Irish politicians turned a blind eye to this practice and ignored British demands that the ports should be closed to them. Ireland was neutral, they said, ignoring the fact that several thousands of their countrymen were serving in the British forces. This caused a furore in the newspapers and there were heavy demands for the British Government to close the ports by force. Debate followed in the house and in one of his famous speeches Winston Churchill said he was of a mind to do just that and close the ports, but when he considered the massive contribution by the Irish servicemen to the war effort – and he mentioned Paddy Finucane, an RAF VC, and L/Cpl Kenneally of the Irish Guards – he could not find it within himself to carry out such a decision. When I heard this speech on the radio I could not help but smile to myself. Taking an Irish name had certainly helped me, so I was glad to help my 'adopted' countrymen in a small way.

Defeat in Europe was becoming a certainty for the Germans and as each squad of reinforcements left I asked repeatedly to be allowed to go with them. I was no glory hunter but wanted to join the few of my old comrades left and be in at the kill. Finally, my Colonel relented and I took a squad of thirty ex-RAF, now soldiers, to join the 3rd Battalion. We travelled by train to Hull and then by boat to Amsterdam. Two days later at a staging camp we heard on the British Forces Network that the German forces had surrendered to General Montgomery at Luneberg Heath. I did not fire another shot in World War II. I had survived.

It took us over three weeks of moving from one staging camp to another and we finally found the battalion in Gummersbach in the Rhineland. In the intervening time events had moved swiftly. The Guards Armoured Division had been stood down and the 3rd Battalion had been disbanded and joined up with the 2nd. For me it was great to be in a service battalion again after six months of strictly disciplined recruit training. I was promoted CQMS and posted to No 2 Company. My CSM was Desmond Lynch, ex-1st Battalion, but he was on extended leave so I had the Company to myself.

Immediate post-war Germany was something else. To the victor the spoils of war and we certainly had our share. Gummersbach was a delightful little town, luckily untouched by the ravages of war. Duties were light and discipline was relaxed; it was a time of rest and rehabilitation. The town was practically devoid of German males between the ages of seventeen and seventy-four; many were killed, wounded or prisoners of war and it was to be some months before they returned in dribs and drabs. There was supposed to be a non-fraternisation ban in force but it was ridiculous and few took any notice of it. On the one hand there were 600 young healthy guardsmen looking for a good time after years of discipline and war; on the other, a town full of young women bereft of male company for years and very willing to give it to them.

Most of us had German girlfriends and indeed quite a few formed relationships that ended in marriage, although the powers-that-be frowned upon these unions. Like their sisters in Britain who became GI brides, many of these German girls found post-war Britain not a lot better than the ravaged Germany they left behind. However, a lot of these marriages lasted and I still count amongst my friends a lot of guys who married German girls and whose marriages have endured for over forty years; these relationships did a lot to bring Britain and Germany together in the following years.

Nothing lasts for ever and we moved from Gummersbach to Wandsbek just outside Hamburg. A lot of girls followed the battalion to their new station. At that time, if a girl had a decent soldier lover she stuck to him; she had to, to survive. Amongst them was my own girlfriend Lisa. I gave her a small fortune in black-market goods and packed her off home; she was only eighteen and she would survive. It was all too easy to get into heavy relationships; I was married and my first son Michael had just been born.

Wandsbek had been the HQ of the Waffen SS and was a very up-to-date barracks. We were put on internal security duties; we supplied guards, road blocks, patrols and even firing squads. Hamburg, as one of Germany's major ports, had been devastated by allied bombing and was in a terrible state. Nineteen-forty-five and the winter of 1946 were terrible times for the German population – thousands were homeless and lived in ruins; there was little food and in the winter no fuel and no clothing; people had to survive on their wits and the black market was rampant. The country was divided into four zones, American, British, French and Russian; when this was announced there was a mass exodus of the civilian population into the British and American zones. This made our task to help them so much harder.

We could not blame the Germans, since the Russian treatment of the populace was absolutely ruthless. Most of the

Russian troops had left for eastern Germany when we arrived in Hamburg but there was a rear party of a Russian infantry outfit left in a block of flats near our barracks. To me they looked like descendants of Ghengis Khan and they acted in the same manner. They were, to a man, absolute bastards. No young woman stood a chance with them and all kept well out of their way. No matter to the Ivans, middle-aged or old ones would do. I saw them strip the boots off fragile old men if they looked in better condition than their own. Another delightful habit was to rip telephones off the walls and stuff them in their kit bags to take home.

Occasionally we would socialise and, boy, could they drink. In our halting conversations I gathered that the German Wehrmacht had treated the Russian populace in a far worse manner than they were treating the Germans. If that were so, they were exacting their revenge in no uncertain manner. I chatted with a lieutenant who had been promoted from the ranks; he was a man of about forty and a real tough cookie. He had been an infantry sergeant at Stalingrad when they drove the Germans back. I told him about the German POWs in North Africa who had been on the Russian front and fired their machine guns at Soviet infantry until they got red hot and seized up, inflicting thousands of casualties. He shrugged and said Joseph Stalin had never concealed the fact that a million lives more or less are of no importance in the big picture. I thought that mentality had died out after the First World War — how wrong I was.

Once the zoning of West Germany had been finalised our Soviet allies, their kit bags stuffed with loot, soon left the British zone, much to the relief of the local populace. The relationship between the American, British and Russian forces after the first flush of victory had always been uneasy and whatever the rights and wrongs of zoning, from an ordinary soldier's point of view the lines had been drawn and we knew where we stood.

The Control Commission was gradually getting into gear and slowly some sort of order began to appear. They were going to need it. That winter of 1945–46 was to be the worst in Germany in living memory. One of our worst headaches were displaced persons, some of whom had formed themselves into gangs and roamed the outlying areas. We called them the werewolves. They looted, raped and killed and were the worst bunch of cut-throats I ever came across. They comprised mainly Eastern Europeans: Poles, Hungarians, Rumanians, Russian army deserters. They were, for the most part, young men and women who had escaped from concentration and forced labour camps. Naturally they were well armed: the only commodity Germany had a glut of was arms and ammunition. Rounding them up was a tricky operation. We were mainly under the command of the military police; the local Provost Major was God and those identified as murderers and rapists were summarily shot. No doubt injustices were done but when one saw the havoc and atrocities these gangs perpetrated, one's conscience was clean. All the same it was good to get back to the Mess at night and drink ourselves stupid to wipe out the memories of the day's work.

A welcome break in the form of the Victory Parade arrived for a lucky half dozen of us chosen to represent the Irish Guards. We were flown from Hamburg to Croydon in a string bag of a Dakota that had seen better days. From Croydon we travelled to Hyde Park, where we were under canvas; every unit of the British Army was represented, including the Anzacs, Canadians, the Indian Army and the Gurkhas.

VE Day dawned fine and sunny and in a massive co-ordinated operation the British Armed Forces moved off to march through the streets of London and pass the various saluting bases in Whitehall and at Buckingham Palace. Luckily enough the Brigade of Guards detachment were preceded by a Guards Band and we were able to march along at our own measured pace. They played all the tunes of glory and I felt the presence and saw the faces of my fallen friends and comrades marching along with me. The crowds cheered and there was often a special cheer as the Guards went by; the Londoners have a special affection for the Brigade. What they thought of a supposedly tough Irish Guards Sergeant wearing a Victoria Cross marching along with tears streaming down his face I'll never know, and I couldn't have cared less. I wept unashamedly. Theirs was the victory and they were entitled to be happy. For me it was a sad day; I grieved for my friends.

The next day we flew back to Hamburg and I was glad to go. The previous night there were parties and celebrations all over London and I went to a few; but I was in too morose a mood to enjoy them. Rationing was at its height and the British, being what they are, shared what little they had with us. Only beer was plentiful but I had never been one to down pints of the stuff; also my tastes had changed. I preferred the good French wines, Dutch and German schnapps, and Russian vodka; there was plenty of that if nothing else in beleaguered Germany.

That winter was a bad period for the Germans, the battalion and myself. I was drinking far too heavily and getting myself into trouble. I was not alone in this; we drank to forget the misery and suffering around us. Most of the older guardsmen who I had served with were getting demobilised and it was impossible just to say 'Cheerio, nice to have known you' to guys you had shared slit trenches with, so there were Sergeants' Mess parties at least twice a week to cheer them on their way. Another factor was that the command of the battalion was changing; we had two or three commanding officers, many senior officers had left, the RSM and Drill Sergeants kept changing and generally discipline became rather lax. The trouble with myself was that I was not a heavy drinker and when I had had more than enough the wildness would come out in me and I would look for trouble: more often than not I would find it.

Things came to a head one frosty night in February 1946. I was at a heavy mess party to bid farewell to one of the CSMs. A couple of the guys who were as bored as I suggested going to a night club in Hamburg. 'We'll thumb a lift into town easy,' they said. I was well lit up and readily agreed. Heading towards the main gate, we passed the MT room. I spotted the big Austin ambulance parked outside. The keys had been left in. Without a second's thought I said, 'Hop in lads, we've got transport.' I drove towards the main gate with no lights. I had spotted that the barrier was up, and if I was lucky I could slip by quietly and be away before the guard would know what was happening.

I was not lucky. The sentry was alert, lowered the barrier and shouted 'halt'. 'Shit,' I thought, put my foot down hard and smashed through the barrier. The sentry jumped to on one side and fired into the air. By the time the rest of the guard tumbled out I was round the corner and away. I was not too worried about this incident; it was very dark and the sentry could not possibly identify who was in the ambulance. What did worry me was the fact that we could not use the vehicle for long; the guard commander would alert the Military Police in Hamburg and they would soon be patrolling the Wandsbek-Hamburg road. We dropped the ambulance in a side street on the outskirts of the city, locked it up so the natives would not vandalise it and walked towards the centre. None too soon – a couple of Military Police jeeps screamed past us heading towards Wandsbek.

We wandered on towards the city centre and stopped at the first bar we came to. It was to be a bad choice. As soon as we walked in I sensed the atmosphere. It was an all-German bar and there were no other troops there. The locals looked as mean a bunch of polecats as you could find in a day's march. It transpired it was the haunt of the local black marketeers and merchant seamen from the docks. We ordered a drink. The best they had to offer, at least to us, was schnapps which was served out of a clay bottle. I think it was 110% proof: real fire water. Four young women came in and made a beeline for us, asking for cigarettes or chocolate. We bought them a drink and, language permitting, did our best to be friendly. I was all for moving on; however, one of my pals took a fancy to one of the girls and we stayed. It was fatal.

After a few laughs and our second drink a youngish German walked in. He went straight up to the bar and punched my pal's new-found friend in the face. There was a silence for a couple of seconds. I think he was the husband, lover or what-have-you of the girl in question. Then they all came at us tooth and claw. All their pent-up frustrations – their defeat in war, their women's penchant for British soldiers, their misery and spite – were vented on we three guardsmen.

Bottles flew, chairs and tables were smashed, and one

guy came at me with the biggest knife I had ever seen. I kicked him in the crutch. There were too many of them for us and we could not get to the door. We were locked up against the bar window so two of us picked up a heavy table; we threw it straight through and dived after it. I was unlucky: the ground was gravel and I landed on my face. My two pals picked me up and we hared off back up the road with the Krauts in hot pursuit. We soon lost them and considered picking up the ambulance and going back in that, but decided against it and limped back to barracks, getting in the back way. We agreed that it had been a fair night out and went our separate ways.

I flopped on my bunk and slept like a log. I was woken by the storeman with a mug of tea. He was aghast when he saw me – and that made two of us. When I looked in the mirror, I saw that I had a shocking gravel rash down the front of my face. I could hardly move from the bumps and bangs I had taken around my body. The previous night I had not felt a thing. Never again, I said to myself, but I was a little late with that good resolution. I went to the Medic Sgt who spent an hour picking out bits of gravel from my face and cleaning me up; he also gave me a shot of his famous hangover cure. I knew I was in trouble. I asked the Medic Sgt to tell the Drill Sgt-in-waiting how I was, and to ask him to see me in my bunk. Luckily for me it happened to be 'Binky' Stewart – an old friend. He came and I told him exactly what had happened.

'I thought it was you who had nicked the ambulance,' he said. 'You were well lit up when you left the mess and it's the sort of crazy thing you would do.' I gave him the keys to the ambulance and told him roughly where it had been left. 'I can arrange with the MT Sgt to get it picked up quietly and with no fuss,' he said, 'but regarding the fracas in the bar we will have to wait and see if there are any repercussions.' He said he would have to tell the RSM and put him in the picture regarding my absence, but he never asked me who my companions were and I did not mention them.

There were repercussions. The RSM came to see me at 11am. He was 'Snags' Kelly of Training Battalion fame, and he was shortly retiring; my sort of trouble was the last thing he wanted. I repeated my story and then he gave me the biggest tongue-lashing I was ever to receive; the expletives were not for family listening and he ended by saying that I should be double marched to the Guardroom, court martialled, busted down to guardsman and made to do extra fatigues for six months. I was not important but the good name of the Irish Guards was.

It appeared that the bar owner had complained to the German Civil Police who had in turn brought in the Military Police. He said his bar had been completely wrecked, all his stock of valuable wines smashed and with his loss of business he was going to lose thousands of marks and he wanted full compensation. All I could remember were a few broken chairs and tables and a smashed window. However, the upshot of the whole affair was that the battalion had to parade at 2pm that day when the bar owner and one of his staff would try to identify the culprits. I was to consider myself under 'open arrest' and stay in my bunk till ordered otherwise; he would arrange for the Medical Officer to come and patch me up. The battalion duly paraded and of course the plaintiff, in the form of the bar owner, got nowhere. He did identify one sergeant but he turned out to be the Sergeant of the Guard on the night in question.

Confined to my bunk for three days, I was ordered to attend Commanding Officer's orders on the fourth day. 'This is it,' I thought. 'I am for the chop.' The CO gave me another dressing down in much the same vein as the RSM though without the bad language. I was given a severe reprimand for behaviour unbecoming a senior non-commissioned officer. I deserved it and I was fortunate; it was a cover-up, not for me but for the Regiment.

For the next month I was a model of regimental virtue and as I was due a fortnight's leave, the Adjutant sent for me and told me that the 1st Battalion was being re-formed, mainly of guardsmen on regular engagements, and there was a possibility they would be going to Palestine. My demobilisation number was on the horizon and he asked me to think about my future whilst on leave – whether to sign on for a further period of service or leave the army.

Not unnaturally, my wife was for my leaving the army.

After five years of marriage it was a question if I had spent over two months with her, and we also had a young son. Whilst on leave I did make an effort and thought that I might join the Police Force. I went to Birmingham City Police HQ and met a Superintendent Brown of B Division; he jumped at the opportunity to sign me up, which amused me somewhat. He thought I would be quite a capture for Birmingham City Police; everything seemed right about me: I was the right age, six feet one, a guardsman used to discipline, without a criminal record and a holder of the Victoria Cross. I was perfect and I almost began to believe the hype myself.

I passed the educational test and they waived the medical. I signed provisional forms to join them when I was demobilised. The Super was very pleasant with his new recruit and asked me to have a drink with him in the Police Mess. I accepted and at the time really thought I would become one of them, but it was not to be.

I returned to Germany still undecided as to what I was going to do. Like so many young men at that time I had had seven years of adventure. I enjoyed soldiering; the army had been a home for me and I owed them everything. I looked at the Barracks notice board and the answer to my problem stared me in the face. Guardsmen willing to sign a five-year engagement and train as a parachutist could join the 1st Guards Parachute Battalion that was being formed. Apply to Battalion HQ.

I did just that. It did not mean I was leaving the Irish Guards, just that I would be attached to the Army Air Corps. It also meant that as I was not substantiated as a CQMS I would have to drop a rank to full Sgt, but what I lost in pay would be made up by the parachutist's extra pay; in any case money never worries a soldier – you always have your bed and board.

I was glad to leave the flesh pots of Germany; I had been drinking far too much and I was unfit. Still, the Paras would put that right for me, and how.

CHAPTER 11

A NEW BEGINNING

Fifteen of us gathered at Colchester Barracks in Essex where we were joined by another thirty-five from the UK. We were a mixture of all five guards regiments and were to be the nucleus of the 1st (Guards) Parachute Battalion. We moved on to Aldershot, the headquarters of the Airborne Division. We were addressed by RSM Lord, an ex-Guardsman himself, who had served with the Paras during their finest years. He told us to forget all about being guardsmen; here drill was not as essential to being a Para soldier as fitness and we were to embark on a physical training course which had been devised to make us as fit, both mentally and physically, as possible. He warned us it would be hard and some would fall by the wayside; he was right. There was a stiff medical examination to start with and we lost three straight away.

We then started six weeks of torture. The Para instructors took a fiendish delight in turning these cocky guardsmen into exhausted wrecks. We ran and ran everywhere; we climbed ropes, walls and buildings; we pushed and pulled heavy logs. The assault course must have been devised by a gorilla. When I tell you that young men with an average age of twenty-five, after showering and cleaning their kit were in bed by 7pm to be rested for their next day's torture, you will get a sense of what it was like.

The worst exercise was what we called 'The Hill'. This consisted of metal poles set in concrete and placed one yard apart going up to a height of sixty feet and ditto on the down side. This obstacle had to be taken at speed – it was the only way to get momentum to climb it. Going down, the weight of the equipment you carried would force you down quicker than you wanted; the mental and physical concentration required to cross this obstacle was vital. One miscalculation and you were in trouble. We had mishaps of course; twisted ankles, pulled muscles and ruptures pulled our numbers down and only thirty-five of us climbed into coaches heading for RAF Upper Hayford to do our actual parachute training. It had been very hard; I had lost half a stone in weight, had not had a drink for nearly two months and best of all I did not want one. We were really fit and hard and could walk through brick walls if asked.

I really enjoyed the training with the RAF. We were divided into 'sticks' (a new word for me) of twelve men, each under an RAF Sgt Instructor. We were fortunate with our man. He was a Jock who had been a despatcher at Arnhem; he had done over 100 jumps himself and really knew his kit. We learnt how to fall from various heights without hurting ourselves; we were taught the mechanics and theory of parachuting: how to kick out of twists and spins, how to control our rigging lines to land where we wanted and how to judge the wind. The eternal question of why American paras had two chutes was answered: it seems ours always opened. The question of 'Roman candles' (which is when the parachute does not open and just flutters above the unfortunate user) was never answered because they had never been able to ask the unfortunate victim why.

We met the girls of the WAAF who packed our chutes. Our lives were in their hands and we treated those ladies like duchesses; they loved it. Our initial jump was to be from a balloon basket at 600 feet; we were each issued with a chute and helped each other with the fitting of the webbing equipment that strapped it to our backs. We checked the release button so we could get out of the harness quickly. We filed up the steps into the basket which was swinging slightly under the balloon; the winches started up and the balloon ascended.

What got me was the silence; it was eerie. When we reached the required height the only thing to be heard was the whistling of the wind and the beating of our own hearts. The instructor removed a piece of the flooring and I realised why they called the balloon basket the 'coffin': the aperture was just that shape. 'Take a look,' he said. The fields below looked like postage stamps; the control tower and hangars were no bigger than Oxo cubes glistening in the sunlight. 'Who's going first?' he said. 'Any volunteers?' No movement from the strained white faces. 'OK,' he said, 'who's the senior NCO?' As one man they all looked at me.

'God,' I thought; I was the senior sergeant by about six months . . .

'Sit at the head of the aperture,' he said, 'and let your legs hang down.' I did just that. He took my parachute static line and hooked it on a bar above me. 'Are you happy with that?' he said. I checked it and croaked, 'Yes.' 'When you are ready, just push yourself off with both hands and away you will go.' I looked down. Christ, it was like committing suicide. I pushed myself off. The wind grabbed me. I was falling, falling. I heard a loud crack above me and felt a sharp tug at my harness. I looked up and there was my canopy billowing open. 'Oh, you beaut,' I shouted and blessed the WAAF packer of my chute. I was lost in the thrill of it all as I drifted down. I heard shouting down below. The instructors on the ground were bellowing at me through a megahorn, the ground was coming up fast and I was way off the whitewashed circle I was supposed to land in. I yanked on my rear rigging lines and hit the ground in a heap just inside the circle.

It was not a very good landing but I would do better. Nothing could take away the euphoria of the moment. It had been a fantastic thrill and like a child I wanted to do it again. All the men felt the same as they came down in quick succession – all bar one. We had a 'jibber', a phrase used by the instructors for a man who refused to jump. He came down in the basket with our instructor. He was put in a truck, taken back to the billets, gathered his kit and packed off back to his unit. You get no second chance in the Paras. I felt terribly sorry for him; it was not easy to make that first jump.

We did a further eight jumps, this time from a Dakota aircraft at varying heights. Speed was of the essence and we would shuffle along the aircraft and stand at the door. 'Red light on'; 'Green light go'. The despatcher would slap you on the back and away we would sail. It was great; the seventh jump was with a heavy weapon or boxes of ammunition in a kit bag. The trick was that once out of the aircraft and with your chute opened, you would lower the kit bag a distance of some forty feet with a rope. The descent was much quicker because of the extra weight but, surprisingly, the landing was easier. When the kit bag hit the ground the loss of weight caused the parachute to brake slightly and the landing was simple. The eighth and last jump of our training was to be carried out at night. This was to be a bit tricky. It was very difficult to judge the ground and one needed every bit of concentration. At the cost of one twisted ankle we all did it.

Next day we attended the passing-out parade and were presented with our parachute wings and red berets. We spent the rest of the day sewing on our insignia, not forgetting to sew a sixpence under our parachute wings for luck. That night there was a station dance and we thanked those beautiful parachute packers in more ways than one. It was without doubt the finest course I ever had in the army.

Back at Aldershot events moved quickly. We were kitted out with khaki drill, visited the regimental tailor, received various medical jabs, issued with railway warrants and passed for seven days' embarkation leave. We were going to join the 1st Para Battalion, part of the 6th Airborne Division in Palestine.

My wife was not amused, to say the least. I had told her I would consider leaving the army and here I was, all dressed up and wearing a red hat, off to foreign parts (as she put it) again. I did my best to placate her. I said I would definitely leave the army when I returned.

Our second son, Shane, was born whilst I was in Palestine. To be perfectly honest, post-war Britain was not a nice place to be. There were shortages of everything, there was a Labour government in power, cutting back on capitalism. Nationalisation was the key word and most people were out for themselves. So it was a buoyant Kenneally that sailed from Southampton. It was the usual old trooper we sailed in. By this time there were cabins for the officers, double-tier bunks for sergeants and above, and the dreaded hammocks for other ranks. The food was good, much better than on my last trip to Africa. We had a Coldstream CSM in charge of us; he had not done Para training but the battalion was short of a Warrant Officer and he had been posted immediately. There were all sorts of units on board; the British army was in a state of flux due to demobilisation and there was a constant stream of troopships criss-crossing the

Mediterranean. The old ship developed an engine fault and we spent three days in Malta while it was repaired. The island had certainly taken a hammering from the Luftwaffe and the air was thick with dust from the demolition and rebuilding work going on. We were allowed ashore but there was not much to do.

A few days later we sailed into Port Said and landed in Egypt. We were to stay in Ismalia for four days before boarding a train to take us into Palestine to join our unit. The CSM, who had been there in 1937, took the opportunity to take six of us into Cairo, visit the Pyramids and have a night on the town. He was a good guy and came from Manchester; he would amuse us greatly by always referring to his wife as the 'Golden Cloud'; we naturally assumed he meant her crowning glory.

I was disappointed with the Pyramids visit. They, of course, were magnificent but the surrounding area was a tip: empty beer bottles, cigarette packets and paper were scattered everywhere, heaps of camel dung abounded and the area stank to high heaven. Another drag were the pestering Egyptian guides: traders, pimps, and hordes of young boys. You could buy anything and they certainly seemed to cater for the baser side of man. There were sinister-looking coshes bound in leather, knuckle-dusters, knives and daggers of every description, dirty postcards, Spanish fly, and love potions that guaranteed that one drop would make the lady of your choice swoon into your arms.

Pimps would cajole us to visit their establishments – all certified young virgins and all tastes catered for. The depravity of it all seemed amusing at first but rapidly provoked disgust. It was an interesting day; the only things we purchased were fly swatters, which were essential.

We ended the day with a visit to a night club and cabaret in Cairo; the drinks were terribly expensive, even the iced water was charged for and our piastres were disappearing fast. It seemed that the only thing free in Cairo was the clap. The cabaret was mediocre but we waited to see the stars of the show – two Turkish belly dancers straight from the Sultan's palace (or so they said). It would appear that the Egyptians and Arabs liked their ladies a little on the plump side – these two certainly were – and as the music wound up to a crescendo the dancers gyrated faster, the audience went wild and showered them with money, and that was it. I cannot say that I was impressed with Cairo and its surroundings.

Early in April 1947 we left by train for Palestine; I say train, but it was an apology for one. It was completely open-sided with hard benches running back-to-back through the centre of the carriages. It was equipped with a chain which we linked through the trigger guards of our arms and the webbing of our packs. This safety precaution was vital, for as we trundled through the Canal Zone and Egypt at a maximum of twenty miles an hour with frequent stops for an over-heating engine, we were invaded by Arab traders selling bread, tomatoes, eggs, drinks, etc. There seemed to be hordes of them and they would steal anything – nothing was too hot or too heavy. Many an unsuspecting soldier saw his kit bag sailing through the air to be picked up by Arab youths running alongside the train. They were the most skilful thieves I ever came across; if they could nick a rifle that was a special bonus: they fetched big piastres.

This nuisance petered out as we left Egypt, crossed the desert of the Negev and headed towards Gaza. We were now in Palestine proper.

At the close of the Second World War the extent of the Nazi 'Final Solution' had become sickeningly clear. Six million Jews with countless others had been systematically murdered by the Nazis and their henchmen all over Europe. For many of the survivors, Palestine, the Promised Land, seemed the only place to turn to. Whilst the sympathy of the world was now unquestionably with the Jews, that alone was not going to further the Jewish cause.

The Arab nations remained implacably opposed to the Jewish state in Palestine. Britain, the mandatory authority, was facing an acute fuel shortage at home and was unwilling to risk its Arab oil interests even though an Anglo-American commission in 1940 had recommended the immediate admission of 100,000 Jewish refugees. Not willing to lose its Arab oil, Britain closed the gates of the Promised Land and they remained firmly barred to the Jews.

Despite this embargo, illegal immigration continued. Stopping it was a heart-breaking and distasteful task but until the United Nations decided on a solution it was the job of the British troops and Palestine Police to keep the two protagonists apart. The period between the end of the war and the 1948 Declaration of Independence by the re-named Israel was brutal, vicious, and extremely violent. Determined to press their case with more strength, the Jews continued to smuggle immigrants into Palestine. Almost every woman of child-bearing age was pregnant – the woman always reckoned on bringing two in. Most of those who landed were captured and sent to internment camps at Famagusta in Cyprus.

At the same time Jewish and Arab terrorists began a campaign of brutal random violence. In one incident the British hanged seven Irgun and Lehi men for these activities (the Irgun and Lehi were terrorist off-shoots of the Jewish National Army which was called the Haganah). In retaliation the Irgun hanged two British sergeants in an orange grove, booby-trapping their bodies which exploded when they were cut down. In one of the most despicable acts of the period the Irgun, led by Menachim Begin (later Prime Minister of Israel), blew up the offices of the British mandatory government in the King David Hotel in Jerusalem. Nine people died – British, Jews and Arabs. To this day Irgun leaders claim they telephoned a warning. Who can believe men who booby-trapped the bodies of executed British soldiers?

Large supplies of weapons, ammunition and military equipment – all the bric-a-brac of World War II battlefields – were illegally smuggled in to arm both factions. Jerusalem, the jewel of Palestine and prized by both Jews and Arabs, suffered badly. An Arab bomb blew up a large area of Ben Yehuda Street, the main street of Jewish Jerusalem, with many lives lost. The Arabs tightened their hold on the city, continually attacking the convoys sent from the coast to relieve the Jewish community. Food and water were rationed. It was at this time, without the knowledge and agreement of their official leaders, that Irgun and Lehi terrorists massacred a great number of the population of Deir Yassin, a large Arab village to the west of Jerusalem. In reprisal the Arabs ambushed and murdered a convoy of doctors and nurses heading to Hadassah Hospital on Mount Scopus.

This, then, was the background to the operations of 6th Airborne Division in the months before the British mandate ended. It was possibly the most hazardous internal security duty carried out by British troops; the opposition, both Jews and Arabs, were clever and utterly ruthless.

We carried on by train from Gaza to Haifa, thence by truck to Tiberias on the Sea of Galilee, where I met up with my new comrades of the 1st Para Battalion. The unit was in a state of change; the CO and RSM were both Coldstreamers, there was only one Drill Sgt, a Grenadier, and there were few junior Guards officers. I was posted to 'R' Company which had a Welsh Guards Company Commander and a Para CSM named Dent, who became a friend. We had no officer platoon commanders. I was given an all-Para platoon; they were mainly National Servicemen who had completed their para training at the end of the war and were serving out their compulsory time. There were a few who had been in action and two who had been at Arnhem – regulars who were coming to the end of their engagements.

At first they regarded me with suspicion but after a couple of weeks they began to enjoy me as I enjoyed them. I think they were tickled to finish their service under an Irish Guards platoon sergeant and a VC to boot. They were very fit, tough and athletic; their weapon training was marvellous, their drill bloody awful. Strangely enough they used to enjoy the drill parades the RSM instigated; they genuinely admired the style and precision of the guardsmen and it was the one area in which I could teach them something. It was very satisfying to have a Para platoon with Irish Guards style. The discipline and spirit was first class and in the year we had together, through some tricky and dangerous incidents, I never had cause to put one man on a charge. To this day I still get the odd letter and phone call from ex-paras of 'R' Company.

Introductions over, the battalion was soon involved in its internal security duties. My first experience was harbour duties in Haifa. Men who had done this duty before warned that it was a shocker. The Palestinian Police convoy came into the dock area carrying almost 400 illegal immigrants with military escort. It was our duty to organise them into groups; they were to have a quick medical inspection, a meal, then were to be loaded into a ship and carried over to Cyprus overnight where we would hand them over to the Military Police for internment. It sounded easy. Security was very tight, we had a machine gun at each end of the dock area, and every access point was heavily guarded: the place was like a steel trap.

They were mostly Eastern European Jews, the majority Polish and Russian. They were in a bad state. Apart from the privations of a voyage from Europe packed in cargo ships with few facilities, they had been dumped on the beaches of southern Palestine and rounded up by the police and military – so much for the Promised Land. The British soldier is not of the stuff the SS troops were made from. We tried to be caring, especially with the old and infirm and, of course, the women and children. They shouted and screamed as if they were being handled by the devil incarnate. The abuse they hurled at us was obvious although we could not understand it. The younger elements among them were very awkward and obstreperous. It was hard to keep calm and patient.

We gave them a meal first, which was occasionally thrown back in the face of the server. One young woman threw a plate at a Glaswegian Para sergeant, splitting his forehead wide open; he had to be held back from felling her on the spot. They goaded us; I think they wanted to accuse us of brutality. The medical examination was the worst point. Each immigrant was quickly examined. Those women who were heavily pregnant and near their time were given the opportunity to go to hospitals in Haifa; they were all for this but when they learned they had to go alone, without their family, they soon rejoined the group. Many of the younger pregnant women did take this chance and of course they were in Palestine to stay.

The flashpoint came when the medics found that 95 per cent of them were lousy with lice; the captain of the transport taking them to Cyprus would not take them aboard until they had been disinfected. We rigged up canvas and hessian screens so that this operation could be carried out with a modicum of decency, especially for the women. It entailed dusting their hair with disinfestation powder and pumping the powder inside the clothes of the men and up the skirts of the women. All this caused another uproar; interpreters tried to tell them what we were doing but they were not having any of it. We had to push them through to the medics shouting and screaming as if they were being tortured.

During the day an American cargo ship had moored in the dock alongside us. The crew were lining the deck rails observing the hullabaloo of the proceedings down below. There was no doubt where their sympathies lay, and it was not with us. They called us Limey bastards and many other sweet obscenities; they also showered us with tins of beans and tomatoes, eggs and rubbish. One young soldier was laid out by a tin of peaches. This was too much for the Para Sgt in charge of a machine gun at the end of the dock. He opened up and used half a belt of ammunition firing just above the water line the length of the ship. This certainly had its desired effect. The Yankee sailors disappeared like rabbits down a hole. Silence reigned till we all cheered the machine gunner; it also quietened our charges, who seemed a little more amenable after the burst of fire.

I don't know what happened to the machine gunner. I would have given him a medal, but knowing the British Army he was probably disciplined and then promoted quietly when the fuss died down. We sailed for Cyprus that evening with the Jews packed tightly all over the ship; we gave them another meal which was accepted this time with a little more grace. We docked at Famagusta in the morning and passed our charges on to the Military Police with no regrets and some relief. The Jews' destination was the internment camp, but not for long; the British would be leaving Palestine and the Promised Land would be theirs.

Whatever the rights and wrongs of the Palestine situation, and it certainly reflects no credit on the British government, we as soldiers were doing our duty as ordered. In my considered opinion the establishment were pro-Arab, but the ordinary soldier could not care less one way or the other. In fact, towards the end of the mandate, the majority of soldiers favoured the Jews. They had suffered so much in Europe; we saw the hardship and misery they went through in Palestine and they were outnumbered ten to one. The ordinary Britisher will always favour the underdog. What did us down were accusations of cruelty and brutality in certain sections of the press; one American writer, Ben Hecht (a Jew), wrote that every time a British soldier was killed he felt a song in his heart. Such rubbish — brutality and torture were practised only by the opposing sides themselves.

Thankfully, no more port duty for us. We were to man roadblocks on the various entrances to Haifa. Each platoon, with a couple of Palestine policemen, searched all vehicles, both Jewish and Arab, for arms, ammunition and hashish, which the Arabs were fond of running. My platoon dropped lucky; we manned a roadblock halfway up Mount Carmel, overlooking the city. It was one of the most beautiful spots in the world: the views out to sea and of the city were magnificent. It was very green and flowery and the scent of jasmine at night was overpowering. This was the upper-class residential area of the city and we were not troubled much. We did dig out a few rifles and pistols which we confiscated. We also caught one young Arab with an urn full of hashish which he insisted was for his Jewish customers. There were numerous incidents on the outskirts of the city and spasmodic exchanges of fire; arson and looting were commonplace. Happily ensconced in the aristocratic heights of Mount Carmel, my platoon was not involved; we were there for three weeks and it was like being on holiday.

The 1st Para Btn was due its annual three-jump refresher course and we moved from Haifa to southern Palestine near the Sinai desert where the jumps were carried out. The nonchalance of the Paras on this exercise impressed me very much. We jumped from no more than 400 feet; the object was speed and more speed from leaving the aircraft, landing and regrouping. It was a piece of cake; there was little or no wind and the air was thin. On each of my three jumps I landed on my feet − brilliant for me, nothing to the members of my platoon who did it every time. Stick after stick tumbled out, were down in seconds, regrouped and marched off. The Company Commander said, 'Well done' − praise indeed.

We moved east to the Transjordan frontier where we camped alongside the Transjordan Frontier Force. This was a cavalry unit of Bedouin Arabs officered and commanded by the British; the officer commanding was known to all as Glubb Pasha. They were caught up in the Labour government's massive defence cuts and were due to be disbanded. We were fortunate enough to be invited to the parade when they were stood down. There are few sights more exciting than watching a light cavalry regiment going through its paces. We watched them go through the canter, gallop and finally the canter past their famous commanding officer for the last time. In their red and white burnouses they looked magnificent. It was sad to watch the end of another chapter of British military history.

CHAPTER 12

PARTING SHOTS

From the Transjordan border we moved north east to northern Galilee, the most troublesome area in Palestine. Bordered on one side by the Lebanon and the other by Syria, it was a spectacularly beautiful area, very fertile and in early spring covered with masses of flowers. For many years it had supported mixed settlements of both Jews and Arabs who had lived in comparative peace. The main road in the area ran from Tiberias in the south to Metulla on the Syrian border in the north. It was estimated that the Arabs had a force of some 3,000 armed men undergoing training in the Golan Heights; these came from Syria and constantly sent down raiding parties to attack the isolated colonies and kibbutzim. Adding to the turmoil, armed gangs of irregulars would infiltrate from southern Lebanon and attack Jewish settlements in Galilee. The main town of the area was Safad, where some 2,000 Jews and 6,000 Palestinian Arabs lived side by side; the Jews were up against it to say the least.

Incident followed incident. Arab attacks were followed by Jewish reprisals and no prisoners were taken. In the middle of this, trying to keep the two factions apart, stood the British soldier and he was not immune from attack. Both sides were on the lookout for arms and ammunition.

Many units were to suffer casualties and the loss of equipment. Security was of the utmost importance.

Each company had an area it was responsible for; within that area the three platoons would come in and the Company Commander would detail this platoon or that platoon to sort it out. If it was a big incident we would be commanded by an officer; in minor ones the platoon sergeant would be responsible. We maintained a 'Trouble Shooter' platoon at all times. This consisted of a 15cwt Bedford truck with extra ammunition, medical supplies, water, etc., with a duty medic available, and two carriers equipped with all the infantryman's paraphernalia: Brens, Stens, grenades, mortars and bombs. We had maps of the area with notorious trouble spots pinpointed.

A call came in – a Jewish bus had been ambushed on the winding Capernum-Safed road. We were duty platoon and off we hared. The picture was all too clear as we came round a bend in the road. The bus was half in the roadside ditch; sheltering behind it were the occupants, Jewish agricultural workers. They had an escort of two Haganah soldiers armed with a couple of old Ross rifles. The driver was still in his seat with a shoulder wound and shattered thigh, and one young woman had a stomach wound. A force of some twenty Arab irregulars were having a field day until we arrived; they were pooping off at everything that moved behind the bus from various points on the overlooking hillside, around three hundred yards away.

Bullets were pinging off the sides of the carriers and we could do nothing to help the bus driver till those Arabs were taken out. I deployed my men along the ditches and opened up with both Brens and rifles. I am a great believer in plenty of 'bang bang' as the Yanks would say – them with the biggest bang wins the war. The lads thoroughly enjoyed the work-out and when the surge of fire had had its effect I had difficulty in restraining them from chasing after the retreating Arabs. It was not my job to take captives or to suffer casualties. The truck with the medic and the wounded was sent to Safad whilst we waited for a replacement bus to arrive. We got no thanks from the Jews. We expected none. Such incidents were commonplace.

There were two sides to the coin. The muktah of a local Palestinian Arab village complained that they had been attacked twice at night in the week. Parties of Jews had infiltrated the village laying explosives: some houses had been demolished and many damaged. Fifteen Arabs had been killed, amongst them women and children. They were frightened to stay there after nightfall so they slept in the surrounding hills and returned at daybreak. It was decided that each platoon would stay at night in the village on guard duty. Our turn came around and we duly moved into the village just before dusk. It was unoccupied except for the muktah's son and his two wives. I suspect they only stayed to see that these heathen soldiers did not steal any of their belongings. The village was a jumble of flat-topped houses and mud huts built round a square of packed earth; they had no perimeter defences and the place was virtually indefensible. My orders were simple. Four men in pairs to be patrolling at all times, the usual two hours on, four off. Anything suspicious, they were to fire straight away; none of this 'Halt: who goes there?' lark. It was not a situation to mess about.

The Arab gave us a large hut for a base. It stank to high heaven, but beggars can't be choosers. He occupied the hut next door. His heavily veiled wives flitted in and out bringing us hot water for our tea and offering Arab flat bread and figs. Dozing dutifully in the small hours I heard a shout and two rifle shots. We grabbed our weapons and ran to the sentries standing on the track that led to the village. 'What's the trouble?' I said. 'I don't know yet, Sarge,' the elder of the two Paras replied. 'We heard what sounded like footsteps coming up the track, we shouted and fired, then nothing.' I looked at him. He was a good soldier, not the jittery type or the sort to let off a round if he was bored; but it does happen. 'OK,' I said, 'keep your wits about you.'

Next morning at sun-up I stretched my aching muscles; the ground had been hard. Opposite me in the corner of the compound one of the Arab wives was squatting urinating. She saw me and in her embarrassment lifted her garibeah right over her head displaying all her charms. It amused me; last night they had both been heavily veiled with only the whites of their eyes visible and here was one exposing everything that nature had endowed her. Not so funny was the donkey we found standing patiently at the end of the village. It had two panniers. One contained a can of water and a ready-made first-aid kit; in the other were sticks of industrial dynamite, lengths of fuse wire and detonators. We checked the houses – nothing. Our sentries must have panicked them with those two shots and they had left the donkey behind.

Another incident occurred when we were on ordinary patrol way past Rosa Pina and almost into Syria. In the distance we could see the snow-covered Mount Hermon and like a bloody fool I went on a few more kilometres so that we could all have a better view. It was beautiful; recently there had been heavy rain and, with the hot spring sun, the flowers on the hillsides were in full bloom. The air was fresh and clean, carrying the scent of the flowers. It really was a most pleasant land.

To my right about a mile away, perched high on a hill, stood one of those white French Foreign Legion Forts surrounded by Arab houses and huts. There were herds of goats grazing and I could see activity around the fort. There were eighteen of us spread through three Bren Gun Carriers. I said, 'Right lads, that's it. Turn around and follow me, we'll head off back.' My driver locked his track and spun round and I led off, expecting the others to follow. One did but the rear carrier, when turning, had skidded on the gravelly road and spun into the ditch. We backed up, stripped the carrier to take the weight off it and the driver tried to extricate it. No good, the track was spinning in the mud and digging itself in. 'Get the tow ropes.'

We did not get the chance to. Hundreds of Arabs were streaming down the hillside from the fort and houses above; they were firing in the air and shouting, obviously geeing themselves up for a fight. Jesus, I thought to myself, we're in trouble. I cursed myself for coming so far out. We would be a great prize for them – three BG carriers, all the automatic weapons and ammunition plus the mortar and bombs. If the Arabs did not shoot me, the army certainly would. They were still coming. That's it, I thought. If they wanted it, they would have to fight for it. I deployed my three Bren gunners, left flank, right flank and one in the centre; the mortar crew I kept by me.

The Arabs were within five hundred yards of us; a few were kneeling down and taking pot shots at us. Bullets were thudding into the carriers and digging into the gravel. Parties of Arabs were peeling off to the left and right. That was the last thing I wanted: if they got round us, we'd had it. I told the Bren gunners to open up, aiming a hundred yards in front of them; the riflemen, too. I did not want them to inflict casualties at this stage. If we could stop this battle before it really started, so much the better. It was the mortar that did the trick; we put four bombs straight in front of them and it stopped them dead in their tracks; they had no cover against that. It was probably the first time they had experienced mortars and it shook them rigid. The firing stopped and the Arabs stayed where they stood.

A party of six detached themselves and came towards us; they were half dressed in military uniforms and wearing the saffron burnouses of the Syrians. The leader came forward and spoke English with a heavy French accent. 'Why did you fire on us?' he said. 'You fired first,' I replied, and pointed at the bullet marks on the sides of the carriers. He was carrying a German Luger on his belt; his comrades were also carrying German Mauser rifles and one had a Schmeisser automatic – they were certainly well armed. 'I thought you were a Jewish force coming to attack us,' he said. 'I have never known Jews wear red berets,' I replied. He dismissed that and he and his comrades looked carefully around.

We both knew that he dearly wanted our equipment but we had too much firepower for them. He mentioned the fact that it was rare for British patrols to venture so near the Syrian border; taking a leaf from his book I dismissed that with a shrug. He asked when the British Army was leaving Palestine. We had been given strict orders not to disclose the fact that we were leaving in May. 'Soon,' I said, 'soon.' 'When you go,' he stated, 'we will drive the Yenudi into the sea and be masters of Palestine.' 'Good luck to you,' I replied. 'Do you need any help getting that vehicle out of the ditch?' he asked. 'No thanks,' I replied. I did not want any Arabs within a hundred yards – what they could not take by force of arms they would certainly steal.

He gave me a cursory nod and signalled his men to go back up the hillside. As they retreated up the hill they started shouting their slogans again and fired into the air as if they were celebrating a victory. They were a bit of a rabble but it had been a close-run thing; my men, as usual, had been terrific, there had been no flap and their professionalism had won the day. We pulled the carrier out and headed back to base. It was with a great sense of relief that I signed the incident book, 'All quiet, nothing to report.'

Entertainment for the troops was practically nil; when time and duties permitted, occasional trips to Jerusalem and Tel Aviv were laid on, but we had to be armed at all times and always in a group. It could be dangerous: neither Jew nor Arab trusted us. The role of peacemaker can be hard. Jerusalem was Jerusalem – full of history, tradition and different cultures – but even in the crisis years of 46–48 commercialism was creeping in. Much more to the taste of the ordinary soldier was Tel Aviv, a newly built city; there were decent bars and cafes and the attitudes of its citizens were completely different to those of Jews in other towns. They had a very modern outlook; all this stress and strife interrupted the desire to get on with their lives and make some money. Not surprisingly, the inhabitants of Tel Aviv were mainly of Western European origin.

Week followed week and as the time we were to leave

Palestine loomed nearer, we became badly stretched in carrying out security duties. We still had to maintain order and attempt to prevent premature uprisings. It was a highly charged situation. Demobilisation was taking its full toll and we were losing men every week. My own platoon was down to eighteen men; I had started with thirty-two. In addition, the Palestine Police were running down, police posts were closing and the men were being repatriated; they had similar responsibilities to us and were equally hard pressed.

Thousands of Arabs were massing on the Lebanon and Syrian frontiers; the Egyptian army and the Jordanian forces were also biding their time. Attacks now became commonplace. The Jewish attacks were carried out with ruthless efficiency and organisation and were all over by the time we arrived. The Arab attacks, on the other hand, were badly managed and took much longer to carry out; consequently the intervening forces would arrive in the middle of a battle. Casualties were inevitable.

My platoon's last duty in northern Galilee was to prove the most memorable. There were two kibbutzes in 'R' Company's area of operations and both were coming under nightly attacks from marauding Arabs crossing from Lebanon. The plan was for a platoon to be put in each one, to advise the kibbutz leaders on defence and repulse any night attacks. Our orders were clear and concise: we were to engage only if fired upon; we must not leave the kibbutz area; if the kibbutz was heavily attacked we were to radio to HQ where the reserve platoon was on standby. We had our usual armaments plus night flares, tracer ammunition and grenades. The company cooks would bring us a hot meal each day with the rations; a duty officer would visit us during the day and night; we were to be there for three days – which turned into ten.

The trucks dropped us and our equipment off at the kibbutz. The CO introduced me to the leader, explained what we were here for and left us to it. Joachim was the leader's name and we immediately hit it off. He was an American Jew from the Brooklyn area of New York. His parents were of Eastern European origin and were victims of the brutal pogroms of the 1880s–1900s. They had bought tickets to New York and emigrated, much like my own grandfather who had a ticket all the way but got off at Hull thinking it was New York. Joachim had left America in 1937 and was one of the founders of this kibbutz. His wife was American but a Gentile and had taken the Jewish faith on marriage. He had a son and a daughter, Rachel, whom I was to meet later. I judged him to be in his late forties. He had served in the Jewish brigade during the war and had some limited military knowledge.

The kibbutz was self supporting, mixing dairy farming with the cultivation of orange groves and figs plus other fruits and vegetables. It was self contained with its own dairy, laundry, carpentry and engineering shops; it even had its own first-aid and medical centre. There were houses for the married couples with children; the young single men and women were housed in long wooden dormitories and they all ate communally. My men were housed in one of these dormitories. Joachim explained that most of the young men were in the hills training with the Haganah for the conflict to come – and no doubt doing a few practice raids on the Arabs, I thought to myself.

The kibbutz was roughly square shaped and covered acres of land. All the main buildings were in the centre; slightly offset was a large water tower on top of which the Jews had built an observation point complete with powerful searchlight. From here Joachim pointed out his problems. One side of the square was covered by orange groves stretching to almost two acres – a battalion of men could have hidden in it. Two sides were used for growing acres of figs and vegetables. The last side, which was also the main entrance to the kibbutz, was fronted by grazing land for the cattle and goats. These were taken out in the morning and herded back in the late afternoon.

There was barbed wire all around the actual area of the buildings, but nowhere near enough of it: a heavy tarpaulin chucked across and you were in. He pointed to the border hills in the distance; bands of Arabs would come down during the day, wait till nightfall, steal up to the wire and open up with rifle and automatic fire. They even had a grenade launcher which caused a lot of casualties and damage. They attacked from all sides and had killed over fifteen members of the kibbutz, some of them women and children.

He had about twenty-two, mainly oldish, men and eight young women who had volunteered to help. There was a collection of old rifles and shotguns; not much ammunition, but plenty of spirit and determination. What could the Paras do to help? It would take a battalion to defend the place properly and cover all points; we could just about defend one side. Time was short; I had to make a decision. I told Joachim to get his carpenters cracking and make fifty large signs with the words 'DANGER – ANTI-PERSONNEL MINES' written in Arabic and Hebrew. These we would space out round the perimeters of the orange groves, fig and vegetable acres, leaving the front of the kibbutz and the grazing fields clear. He remonstrated and said, 'But we have no mines.' 'Neither have we,' I told him, 'but the Arabs don't know that. Don't tell me we are not under observation from the hills. My men will dig the signs in; the Arabs will think they are laying mines. If they do attack we want them to come in on one front and we should be able to handle that; meanwhile, there is tonight to worry about. We'll have to organise guards and patrols with your people.' It was then that I met his daughter Rachel. She was tall and looked about eighteen. She was wearing the usual kibbutz gear – a shirt and very short shorts – which made her long tanned legs go on for ever: a beautiful girl with that touch of arrogance that all attractive girls have. She was to act as interpreter as most of the kibbutz members spoke only Hebrew. Her attitude was cold and wary. She was obviously not thrilled at having to work with the British, and a Para sergeant at that.

Time was short. Dusk was approaching and we quickly worked out a rota of patrols and guards to cover the hours of darkness. It was relatively simple: two sentries at the main gate, a soldier and a Jew, male or female; a sentry at each corner, soldier, Jew alternately; two patrols each starting from the main gate, one to the left, one to the right. It took close on an hour to cover the whole perimeter; they would cross at the halfway point, checking each sentry as they passed. I took my turn as did Joachim. I teamed up with Rachel, he with my Lance Sergeant; this way we covered the whole area and no sentry was alone for more than fifteen minutes.

Rachel and I talked desultorily as we took our turn to patrol; she carried a Lee Enfield rifle and a bandolier. I teased her gently as to whether she could shoot and was informed stiffly that she had spent a month with the Jewish Defence Force learning to do just that. When I informed her that I was half Jew myself her attitude visibly softened towards me and she became much more animated: she was half-and-half herself. During my two patrol stations with her I learnt a lot about Rachel, about her family, the hopes and aspirations of the Jews, their determination and resolve to stay in Palestine and create the new state of Israel; it was a new name to me then. It was a peaceful night, thankfully, for the new day was to be a busy one. The kibbutz cooks supplied us with tea and coffee. They were not too thrilled with the soldiers cooking their own bacon, as they were strictly kosher. We had a laugh: when one of the lads offered a slice to the ever-watching children, a mother snatched the child away.

Everyone went to work with a will. Joachim had been as good as his word; the carpenters had worked all night and produced the signs I wanted. The signwriter had added a skull and crossbones logo above the Arabic and Hebrew warnings – they looked most sinister. With Jewish help, we dug them in round three sides of the perimeter whilst the paint was still wet.

The CO and CSM came up with rations and the mail. The signs intrigued him; he thought it was a good idea and would pass it on to the other kibbutz. Intelligence reports indicated intense Arab activity in the nearby hills. He was of the opinion that one or both of the kibbutzes would be attacked in the next day or so. He advised me where to put the weapon pits, what arcs of fire to use, etc. Joachim, who I had learned was very political, wanted to know why, if the British knew the Arabs had infiltrated into Palestine territory, did they not force them back across the borders before they could attack. He was coldly informed that it was not in the British army's area of operations to attack the Arabs; we were a peace-keeping force, there for internal security and to protect civilian men, women and children. Joachim insisted we were not keeping to the terms of the mandate. The CO dismissed him and would not argue.

When he left we carried on digging weapon pits for the riflemen and set up emplacements for the Brens to cover the whole wire with fixed lines of fire. We sand-bagged the OP on the water tower and I put a Bren up there. There was already an underground shelter for the women and children which was quite substantial. Everybody worked and helped including the children. Rachel was invaluable in interpreting what we wanted and where we wanted it. Joachim was a tower of strength. He realised that we were not the British government, which he despised, but soldiers who were trying to help and willing to put their own lives on the line in so doing. In two days a fine rapport had built up between the soldiers and the people. They appreciated what we were trying to do and we admired them for their single-mindedness and wholehearted assistance.

We worked out our plans. No lights during the hours of darkness. In the event of an attack, women and children into the shelter, men and women who were armed to go to designated weapon pits with a soldier in charge. The soldiers already knew what to do. We had done almost everything we could and I felt confident.

A couple of hours before Rachel and I were due to go out on patrol, Joachim invited me to dinner at his family house. His wife was a wonderful cook and we downed three bottles of Chablis. He told me his family history; how, in the depressed thirties, he and his brother with their families had emigrated to Palestine under the immigration quota. Joachim, his wife, his son Benjamin, and Rachel had joined the kibbutz in its infancy. Benjamin was serving with the Haganah; his brother, who was a motor engineer, had moved to Jerusalem and had a business servicing heavy vehicles and tractors. He was very proud of the fact that they all still had American citizenship.

He asked me to tell him about myself. He was very interested in what Germany was like after the war, and had I met any Jews? I hadn't; to be brutally honest, there were not many left. He asked about British Jewry and I told him they were mainly big-time and doing very well, which was true. How many poor Jews do you see? My family background interested him; he did not know the name Blond. He said it must be a derivation of Blondinsky or something like that. He knew I had a Victoria Cross: he had obviously talked to the other Paras. As I have said, I quite liked him. He was an idealist, but not a starry-eyed one. It was after that evening meal that he set out to subvert me.

Rachel had been a very interested listener during our conversation. Whilst on patrol I asked her about her boyfriends; she did not have a steady one; most of the young men were away with the Haganah. Her previous coldness had completely gone; I think she fancied me a little. I certainly fancied her. On our walks in the darkness we came closer. It was another quiet night and we hoped our presence had warned the Arabs off. I expected the Company Commander would move us back to base; however, he was worried by the continued Arab activity and decided we should stay for a few more days. It was to be a wise decision.

There was no moon that night and the Arabs chose to attack. It was just gone midnight, I had come off patrol and had flopped in my bunk. The sentries' orders were clear: if they heard or saw movement they were to send up a flare. If their fears were realised the klaxon alarm was to be sounded and they were to open fire. The whole kibbutz was to rush to prepared positions and bang away in their arcs of fire; they would cease fire when they saw a green Very light.

The sentry had seen them at a distance of some seventy yards. That yardage was to prove vital. While they rushed the wire, dropped down and started firing, we sped to the weapon pits and opened up; it was just about a dead heat. Whilst the searchlight lasted, which was about three minutes, I estimated there were about a hundred of them in small groups spread along the wire frontage. There was no fire from the rear or from the flanks; the mine warning signs had worked.

Their firing was wild, inaccurate and ill-directed, mainly going up into the thin air. They were using rifles and automatic weapons; no machine-guns. They were using a grenade launcher which again was ill-directed; the only damage it caused was to the side of the dairy. With the light of the flares we pumped up, the riflemen, both soldiers and Jewish men and women, took out the grenade launchers. Meanwhile the Brens on their fixed lines were sending tracer screaming through the wire. It was like a firework display, what with the exploding flares and the tracer bullets pinging off the wire and steel posts, sending up showers of sparks. The whole engagement did not last more than ten minutes. In the light of a flare I saw them retreating in some disorder. I fired the green Very light signal to cease fire. One or two of the more enthusiastic Jews kept banging away but they soon stopped.

We listened carefully. We heard the groans and sobs of wounded Arabs on the wire perimeter. In the distance we heard firing; the tat tat tat of the Brens was very clear. They must have attacked the other kibbutz at the same time. It soon quietened down. The Jews were all for going outside the wire to see what damage they had inflicted and to bring in the wounded, or so they said. I forbade it; no one was to leave the kibbutz until daylight. Perhaps I was being over cautious but it was possible that it was just what the Arabs wanted: to catch us in the open. I need not have worried – they were not good soldiers. Nevertheless, the wounded had to suffer for my decision.

We had just three casualties; one elderly Jew too slow to get to his dugout had been shot in the shoulder; the

Jewish searchlight operator had been cut with flying glass; and one Para had lost the lobe of an ear — he was very lucky. The dairy was damaged; broken glass and splinters of wood were everywhere. A grenade had landed in the goats' corral and quite a number were dead and dying, but that was it — we had been fortunate.

At first light, with a strong escort of both Paras and Jews, we went out and checked the perimeter. There were sixteen Arabs dead and three wounded. The herdsman found two more dead, about half a mile away; these must have been dropped by their fleeing comrades and died of their wounds. So they had lost twenty-one. Most of them had been killed by the Brens: the tracer burns were clearly visible. Those at the foot of the wire were peppered with bullet holes and shotgun pellets. Joachim said they were Lebanese Fellaheen plus three officer types. I was most interested in the arms and ammunition they had dropped in their panic; there was an odd mixture — British, American and German rifles and two boxes of .303 and 9mm ammunition. The American grenade launcher was there plus a box of grenades; most of them carried those fancy Arabian carved daggers as well. I detailed my men to collect all the arms and ammo and lock them up in the ammunition hut.

Meanwhile the Jews were loading the dead on to a flat platform lorry. I went to see what they were doing with the wounded. The three of them had their throats cut from ear to ear. My innate British sense of fair play recoiled at this treatment of defenceless men. I remonstrated with Joachim, who denied any knowledge of who had executed them. He dismissed the incident with a shrug and said if the Arabs had the Jews in a similar position they would have faced a far worse fate. I allowed my men to keep the fancy daggers for souvenirs, together with the odd wrist watch and Palestinian money I was not interested in. Soldiers will be soldiers; I was still wearing that German sniper's watch from Anzio. The men did give me a brand new Beretta 9mm automatic pistol they had found on the Arab officer, complete with holster and spare clips.

The CO came to visit us. He had had a busy night; the other kibbutz had been attacked and so had the base camp. Two Paras had been killed and three wounded. He asked if there were any Arab wounded. I shook my head. 'Surprising,' he said. Arab activity was increasing and orders from 6th Airborne Division were such that we were to stay in position till the last minute, then the whole Division would move to Haifa transit camp. He congratulated the men on doing a good job and warned us to keep alert – he did not want any more casualties. The kibbutz had a celebratory dinner that night in the communal dining hall, soldiers and Jews sitting down together (an unheard-of event). The food was good and the wine flowed. We had not relaxed our vigilance; the guard and patrols were out as usual. After dinner there was music and dancing. They had some great musicians; they sang mournful Russian songs and the live-lier Hebrew ballads went down well. Individuals did various Russian and Hungarian dances. The soldiers introduced them to jitterbugging, which they had learned from the Yanks. It was a good evening; the Jews are a cultured race and I felt myself coming closer to them.

In the small hours Rachel came to my bunk. It was the first time for her and I was gentle. During the ensuing days I had many long conversations with Joachim. He made me a surprising offer. We had talked of what I was going to do when I returned to England. I was undecided whether to stay in the army or go into civilian life. In any case, I had almost three years of my engagement to serve. 'Don't go back, stay here in Palestine with us, stay and help us defeat the Arabs, and build a permanent home for all Jewry.' He looked me straight in the eyes. 'You are as much a Jew as Rachel, Israel could be your home as it is hers.' He missed nothing and knew everything. Two of my soldiers had formed attachments with Jewish girls – it was only natural when young men and women are thrown together in exciting situations. It is a good thing we are leaving soon, I thought, or the Paras are going to be a few soldiers short.

I knew my responsibility: I had a wife and two children at home. I could not just walk away and leave them to it; if I were to become a deserter they would get nothing. He countered this by saying they would deposit £2,000 (later upped to £3,000) in our bank account in England. In 1948 that was a hell of a lot of money and would give anyone a good start. I would be given a Jewish name and sent to the Haganah where, with my military expertise, I would start at least with the rank of a captain and who knew, with good fortune, what rank I could climb to.

'I swear to you, John,' he said, 'we want you as a Jew, not as a mercenary soldier.' (There were British soldiers, though not many, of all ranks who stayed behind in Palestine and served the Jewish cause as paid mercenary soldiers.) 'You owe the British Government and the army nothing. You have served them well,' he said. 'Now is the time to serve your own people.' It was a tempting offer and I agonised over my decision in Rachel's loving arms.

The decision seemed easy but in the cold light of day it was a different matter. To Rachel's credit she did not try to sway me. 'You must do what you have to do,' she said, 'but if you decide to stay in Palestine I will be here for you.'

Desert the army for a second time – how could I even think about it? But I did, and tried to sort out the pros and cons in my mind. In the past I had been a touch ashamed of my half-Jewish pedigree but no more, by God, no more. I had only spent a few days with them, but I felt I had known them all my life. Would I survive the coming of all-out war with the Arab nations where the Jews would be heavily outnumbered? That did not worry me; with stout-hearted comrades I had fought the best and survived. That was the key – the Arabs were not the best; they fought on their nerves and needed to be hyped up. The Jews were disciplined and fighting for their very existence; they did not waiver under fire. It came as no surprise to me that they routed the Arab forces in the two wars that would follow.

I thought of my parent regiment, of my comrades, the Dempseys and Murphys and many others who had given their lives in North Africa, on the Anzio beaches and through Europe; of Gundel and Captain Chesterton who had been an inspiration to us all: great Irish Guardsmen.

The words of old Colonel 'Black Fitz' came back to me. 'Wherever you go, Kenneally, you will be a representative of the regiment. I expect you to behave as such.' Finally, I thought of the new recruits at the Guards Depot learning the names of the regiment's heroes. Kenneally VC – 'Oh yes, he was the bloke who went over to the Jews in Palestine.' I could not do it. I still had that devil-may-care attitude, but to cast a slur on the regiment – no, not even a rogue like me.

The Arabs were very quiet and we had no further attacks; they were obviously waiting for the soldiers to leave before they recommenced proceedings. I kept my decision to myself until the day before we were due to leave. That was to be on 10th May. The Mandate ended on 14th May 1948. I told Joachim while we patrolled the perimeter together. Although disappointed, he understood my reasons. He suggested that once back in England I could purchase my discharge and come to Israel as a private citizen. I would be welcome and he would see to my welfare. 'There is something I can do for you,' I said, and tossed him the key to the ammunition hut. 'Take all those Arab weapons we captured, and the spare ammunition as well; they will help in your defence. I can easily account for them if anyone asks questions.' He was extremely grateful – how grateful, I was to find out later.

The family invited me for a last dinner together. Rachel was very withdrawn, and I was surprised when she came to me in the night. Early next morning the truck rolled up to take us back to base. Rachel gave me a gold tie pin with the word *Mispah* engraved on it. It is a Hebrew word and means love. Like most soldiers I had nothing to give. She had always admired my German watch so I gave her that, plus the small Beretta that the lads had acquired off the Arabs; with the hazardous times she was going to face, it might come in useful. The whole kibbutz turned out to see us off; there were quite a few sad farewells. Just before we drove away, Joachim pushed a stiff brown envelope into my hands. 'Open that in a private moment, John.' We drove back to base, every man jack of us worried about the future welfare of the kibbutz. So much for the uncaring British.

Back at base we met up with the rest of the battalion. We were only just over three hundred strong. They all had stories to tell and their experiences were much the same as our own. In the back of an empty truck I opened the envelope Joachim had given me; inside were one hundred white British five pound notes and a letter. 'John, this is a gift from the kibbutz in thanks for what you have done for us. We now have the confidence to conduct our own defence. If you decide to return I have enclosed an address in Haifa for you to go to; they will look after you and contact me. Shalom.' Rachel had added a postscript: 'Come back Johnny.'

In complete darkness the battalion slipped away like thieves in the night heading towards Haifa. Leaving both the Jews and Arabs to their fate, we did not feel proud. We were to be among the last troops to leave Palestine, along with the rear guards of the Palestinian Police. The next couple of days were very hectic. The Bay of Haifa was crammed with ships and we spent our time loading what we could; only personal arms were to be taken aboard. There was not room for a lot of heavy transport, mortars, ammunition and tons of military equipment. This was all loaded into the vehicles and carriers and driven to the high cliffs which dominated the bay. The handbrakes were taken off and we pushed them over.

We were slinking away from Palestine like a defeated army. The British government's handling of the Palestine question left a lot to be desired. Our last night in the transit camp was noisy, and that is the understatement of the year. Any old soldier who happened to be in that camp will remember it well. The camp was packed with the rearguard units of most of the British Army plus the service corps and the

Palestine Police. My company was one of several on guard duty round the camp. About midnight someone fired a tracer bullet into the air. As if that was a general signal, every soldier started firing into the air accompanied by shouting and cheering. It was infectious. There must have been over 2,000 troops in the area. The noise was horrific, like El Alamein all over again. The officers were running around screaming for the guards on duty to turn out. That was us, but there was nothing we could do, or wanted to do for that matter.

It was highly dangerous fun. Discipline went out of the window; thousands of rounds were being fired into the air. A funny moment occurred: as we were turning out, an infantry officer was shouting for the Sergeant of the Guard. A voice came from one of the bell tents: 'When you find him, ask him to give me an early call. I'm off home tomorrow.' The officer went berserk. 'Find that man, find that man,' he screamed. We dutifully ran round in circles, giggling amongst ourselves.

I think the riot – and it was a riot – was caused by the troops' frustration and their relief to be getting out of the country. We had all seen and helped in the disposal of our equipment over the cliffs. What did a few more thousands of rounds matter? The mood lasted about twenty minutes, then the firing petered out. To their credit the British soldiers had shown what they thought of our ignominious retreat from Palestine and there was nothing at all that the top brass could do about it.

At noon next day, 14th May, we boarded our transport, the SS *Empress of Australia*. We were packed in like sardines and we sailed at dusk. This same day, as the last British troops were evacuated, the Provisional Government under the leadership of David Ben Gurion gathered in Tel Aviv and signed Israel's Declaration of Independence. The new state of Israel had been born. As we sailed out of Haifa Bay the Egyptian air force bombed Tel Aviv. The Arab invasion had begun.

The story of Israel's War of Independence is world history now but suffice it for me to say that by the final cease-fire in early 1949, to the amazement of most, but not to those who knew the Jews, they had not only beaten off the Arab armies who had openly boasted they would drive the Jews into the sea within a week, but they had expanded their own territories far beyond the original boundaries laid down by the United Nations.

The voyage home was uneventful except for the fact that we all got lousy. We were closely packed aboard and with the hot Mediterranean sun the lice had a field day. We all had our heads shaved and the hair from our bodies had to be removed, too, even pubic hair. We lay around the decks near naked wearing balaclavas on our bald heads to prevent sunstroke. We looked like plucked chickens. I won a stack of money playing brag and poker. We landed at Southampton and were immediately given fourteen days' leave. The Paras were ordered to report back to Aldershot, the guardsmen

259

to Pirbright. At the time I thought nothing of those orders, but they were to prove ominous. I said goodbye to the remnants of my platoon; most of them were leaving the army. It had been great serving with them; the Paras were second to none as soldiers. So, sporting a good suntan, very little hair, but loaded with money, I headed to the Black Country to see my second son for the first time.

I spent an enjoyable disembarkation leave and met my new son. He was all fair hair and blue eyes with a cheeky smile: a real chip off the old block; he was to grow up to be one too. My wife was adamant I leave the army. Most of her friends' husbands had been home for a couple of years or more. She had had enough of coping on her own and she more or less presented me with an ultimatum: finish with the army or don't come back at all. I procrastinated and said I only had a couple more years to serve. She countered that: 'I've made enquiries. You can buy yourself out. You have more than enough money.' She was a wife of the old school: in ninety nine cases out of a hundred she went along with my decisions but on this point she was adamant. I half suspected that she knew I had been untrue to her. I was a soldier and lived a fairly dangerous life and took my fun where I found it; she had married me as a soldier and accepted that. She had a different set of moral values to me. To her, marriage was sacrosanct; she had been a faithful wife through the war years and after. Now she wanted a husband at home.

I returned to Pirbright Camp with an unsettled mind and to great changes. Due to massive defence cuts the British Army was going on a peacetime footing. There were big cutbacks in the Brigade of Guards. The Irish Guards were back to one battalion, the 1st, who were stationed in Tripoli with another couple of years to serve in the Middle East. 1st (Guards) Parachute Battalion was to be cut back to a company and renamed the Independent Guards Parachute Company; there would be stringent medical and aptitude tests. Those who failed the medical would be discharged; those who failed the other tests would be posted back to duty with their various regiments. I passed the medical but did not have to take the other tests as I was already a trained parachutist.

Still in an unsettled state of mind I haunted the orderly room to find out what was happening. I was on the list for the Parachute Company and, when everything was organised, would be going to Germany for a three-year tour. That was it — decision time. I had to make my mind up. I did not want to go to Germany; I had had a drink problem out there. From returning soldiers I learnt it was much the same: wine, women and song and no married quarters. Another alternative was to rejoin the 1st Battalion in Tripoli — heat and flies, and no married quarters there either.

I took my problem to the only Irish Guards Officer left in the Parachute Battalion — Major Hendry. I had marched many a mile behind him when he was weapons and tactics officer at the old training battalion. I told him I wanted a couple of years stationed in England to give my marriage a chance. He advised me to see the Camp Commandant and see if I could be extra-regimentally employed in England where a married quarter would go with the job. I could not have picked a worse Camp Commandant to see if I had tried.

He was a whisky-soaked half Colonel of the Grenadiers and looked as if he had spent his war at a desk in the War Office. He spoke to me in a cut-glass accent right out of the top drawer, only in his case it was off the mantelpiece above it. He spoke to me as if I was a recalcitrant schoolboy. He said, 'The run is over now, Kenneally, and you must settle down to proper regimental soldiering. You are twenty-seven years old and we want you to pass on your experience and expertise to the young guardsmen. I see you are to go to the newly formed Parachute Company and on to Germany. You have the choice – it's either that or rejoin your Regiment in Tripoli. There is no possibility of you being employed in England. Those jobs are for non-commissioned officers with much more service than you. Have you anything to say?'

I disliked him and to be fair it was probably mutual; I was not his type of soldier at all. 'If that is the position, Sir,' I said, 'may I apply to purchase my discharge for the rest of my engagement?' He gave me a withering look and said, 'I think you are being impulsive.' With veiled sarcasm he added, 'I think you will find it difficult to express your talents in civilian life. However, today is Friday. Think about it over the weekend and if you still want to follow this course, report to the Paymaster on Monday and then to the orderly room where your discharge papers will be prepared.'

I went home for the weekend. My wife was thrilled at my news and happily pressed a suit and shirt for me to take back with me. I returned on the Sunday night and went to the Sergeants' Mess for a drink. I was in a despondent mood. I did not know a soul among this young new breed of sergeants. They all looked so keen and promotion-happy. How I longed for the company of my old friends and comrades but they were gone. I did not want to be a part of this new army; it was time for me to go . . .

The next day I reported to the Paymaster and we had a settling up. It cost me £120 to purchase my discharge. I had drawn very little pay whilst in Palestine – there had been no need – and it only made a little dent in my money. There was the £500 that Joachim had given me (Israel was an ever-open door for me), also I had the money I had won playing cards on the *Empress of Australia*. I was not leaving the Army penniless. The Paymaster gave me a receipt and asked if I had civilian clothes. I nodded and he told me to get changed and hand all my uniform and kit into the stores, get a receipt for them and take both receipts to the orderly room where I would get my discharge papers. It was all very cold and formal; the army does not take kindly to men who do not complete their engagements. I kept my red beret, parachute wings and medal ribbons. I had earned them.

Dressed in civilian clothes I went to the orderly room and picked up my papers; these were interesting and the Army had the last laugh. When a soldier leaves the army he is given a character assessment to enable him to get employment; there are four grades of these. 'Exemplary', which means you have been a perfect soldier. 'Very Good', meaning not quite perfect. 'Good' (his charge sheets would make interesting reading), and 'Discharge with Ignominy', which means you ain't no good at all. It would be fair to say that 99 per cent of all full sergeants leaving the Brigade of Guards would come out under an Exemplary character, but not yours truly. This is what they had to say:

REGT OR CORPS: IRISH GUARDS ATTACHED ARMY AIR CORPS
ARMY NO: 2722925, RANK: SGT, NAME: KENNEALLY VC
J.P.
MILITARY CONDUCT: VERY GOOD
TESTIMONIAL: A first class non-commissioned who works best when left on his own. In moments of crisis he keeps his head and is capable of using his own judgment. He is always smart and well turned out and sets a good example to his subordinates. He has a good sense of responsibility and leadership.
OFFICERS SIG: J.H. HENDRY. MAJOR IRISH GUARDS

They could have given me Exemplary. It would have cost them nothing. On second thoughts, fair enough – I had not been perfect.

I paused for a few moments and watched the young guardsmen drilling on the square; they were not too bad. As I walked out of the camp passing the two sentries, who did not even acknowledge me in my civilian clothes, I felt like a defrocked priest or as if I had been drummed out. There had not even been a handshake or a 'Good Luck'.

Nearing the station I heard 'Taps' on the bugle for the next parade. For one glorious moment I felt the presence of my old comrades. 'Come on Johnny, it ain't the end of the world.' My resilience returned and I boarded the train heading for adventures new. Sitting quietly, an odd thought struck me – it was the first time in ten years I had paid my own fare home.

I had something to thank King and Country for

JOHN KENNEALLY, VC (1921–2000)

To be a non-commissioned officer with a Victoria Cross – to have superiors obliged to salute when one passes – is to be in a singular, and potentially awkward position. The egalitarian inspiration behind the creation of the VC – as a medal available to individuals of any rank, for acts of outstanding courage – could be at odds with the hierarchical traditions of the Army. Kenneally always felt, and maintained, that his VC was an honour for the Guards. (Had he known, at the time, about the Cabinet-level discussions as to whether he should be kept out of the front line during the latter stages of the war – lest the Germans score a propaganda victory by killing one of the few living holders of the VC – he would have been aghast.)

Modest (though no 'modest fool') in his self-assessment, he remained somewhat insouciant about the wider public acclaim and fame brought by his VC (as well as a little alarmed at the possibility that his assumed identity would be 'rumbled'). His affection for the Guards would only increase over the years, however; and he would receive the signal honour of being one of the few persons not of Royal blood ever to present the shamrock to the regiment at the Saint Patrick's Day parade.

*   *   *

After the war, he worked in the motor industry and, later in life, as a security guard. After his first marriage to Elsie Francis, by whom he had two sons, Michael and Shane, ended, he was to marry Elizabeth Evelyn, a divorcée with a child of her own, Timothy, and to have four more children by her: Martin, Joanne, John and James (who died in infancy). Martin, to whom he dedicated his memoirs, died tragically young in a motor accident in 1981: the writing of his memoirs was prompted by this experience of bereavement.

He would become, over the years, more comfortable with his position of distinction, particularly valuing the opportunities it brought to attend reunions of VC winners, and events commemorating and honouring those who fought and sacrificed so much in the Second World War. He died, aged seventy-nine, in 2000.

John Kenneally having his portrait painted by
Captain H.M. Carr, shortly after winning his VC. The painting
was to hang in the Imperial War Museum for many years

A portrayal of John Kenneally's VC-winning attack,
from the *Illustrated London News*, 1943

'Great Men, Great Guns',
in *Battle Picture Weekly*, 1976

John Kenneally as a young man at the
Saint Patrick's Day parade

Distributing Queen Elizabeth's gift of shamrock to the Irish
Guards at Wellington Barracks, Saint Patrick's Day, 1998

Leading the march to the Guards Memorial,
Saint Patrick's Day, 1998

Meeting the Prince of Wales

John and Elizabeth Kenneally, meeting
the Duke of Edinburgh

John Kenneally, with his granddaughter Katharine